THE
PARENTS' FINANCIAL
SURVIVAL GUIDE

REVISED EDITION

Theodore E. Hughes
and
David Klein

Facts On File®

AN INFOBASE HOLDINGS COMPANY

Also by Theodore E. Hughes and David Klein

- *The Executor's Handbook: A Step-by-Step
Guide to Settling an Estate*

- *Own It and Keep It: How to Reduce Your Taxes, Preserve Your
Assets and Protect Your Survivors*

The Parents' Financial Survival Guide: Revised Edition

Copyright © 1995 by Theodore E. Hughes and David Klein

Facts On File, Inc.
460 Park Avenue South
New York NY 10016

Library of Congress Cataloging-in-Publication Data

Hughes, Theodore E.
The parents' financial survival guide / Theodore E. Hughes and David Klein.
— Rev. ed.
p. cm.
Includes index.
ISBN 0-8160-3278-5
1. Parents—Finance, Personal. 2. Parenting. I. Klein, David,
1919–   . I. Title.
HG179.H84 1995
332.024'0431—dc20   94-23873

Facts On File books are available at special discounts when purchased in
bulk quantities for businesses, associations, institutions, or sales promotions.
Please call our Special Sales Department in New York at 212/683-2244 or
800/322-8755.

Jacket design by M.R.P. Design

Printed in the United States of America

MP FOF 10 9 8 7 6 5 4 3 2 1

This book is printed on acid-free paper.

For the Hughes children

Jennifer and Suzanne

and the Klein children

Helen and Edith

who turned out to be not only affordable

but wonderfully worth it.

CONTENTS

TABLES

WELCOME TO THE CLUB

We'd considered beginning this book with something like "Congratulations! You have just acquired the latest model of *homo sapiens,* and a few hours spent in reading these instructions will increase the many years of pleasure and satisfaction you can expect from this excellent product."

But our second thoughts gave us pause. After all, you've already enjoyed plenty of congratulations—from friends and neighbors, who have no financial responsibility for your child (and who may have been thinking, "Better you than me!") and from doting parents and in-laws, who see the child purely as an emotional asset and not as a financial liability. Instead of congratulations, then, what we would prefer to express is the wish that on your personal balance sheet for the next decade or two the emotional assets that your child represents will outweigh the inevitable financial liability.

Although these two sides of the ledger seem unrelated to each other, actually they're not—but their relationship isn't a simple one. Of course, constant worry about "where's the money going to come from" can dilute the pride and pleasure that your children normally provide, and it may even cause you to resent them now and then. On the other hand, many affluent parents who have no money worries but give their children generous allowances as a substitute for love and attention generally harvest more disappointment than happiness. Emotional satisfaction seems to depend, then, not on the *amount* of money that parents have but on the care, foresight, and ingenuity with which they use it.

What we hope to do in the chapters that follow is to show you how to manage the financial liabilities in ways that keep the value of the emotional assets just as high as possible. But you may also discover that watching your nest egg grow, or managing successfully on a limited budget, also provides you with considerable emotional gratification.

THE NET VALUE OF CHILDREN

Children were not always a drain on the family budget. In fact, from the beginnings of human society until only a century ago, children—especially male children—were seen as a blue-chip investment, and the Old Testament injunction to be fruitful and multiply was probably sounder advice than anything you'd find in today's *Wall Street Journal*.

The reasons were obvious. In a low-technology society, where production depended entirely on human labor, much of it unskilled, a child was able to produce what Karl Marx called "surplus value" by the time he or she was five years old. On the farm, he could herd and feed the livestock, and in only a few years he could help milk the cows and plow the fields. His sister, at the same age, could harvest the beans, husk the corn, and help with the household chores. In the coal mines their small size enabled eight-year-olds of either sex to crawl into tunnels inaccessible to their elders, and in the factories they could make their way between the belts and pulleys to adjust and repair the spinning and weaving machinery. In short, in an agricultural society with almost unlimited natural resources, children were an invaluable source of labor, and in the early days of the Industrial Revolution, most children beyond infancy were wage-earners and contributors to the family's domestic economy.

Even when the young child's asset value was diminished by child labor laws and more sophisticated machinery, it remained high by virtue of his family membership. Male or female, the child did chores on the family farm or assisted in the family business and helped to run what was a low-tech household. Sons and daughters who worked outside the home usually lived at home until marriage and contributed to the household budget in return for room and board. And, because pension plans and Social Security were unheard of, it was taken for granted that children would support their parents in their old age.

Today, of course, all this has changed. To begin with, schooling has escalated from the five or six years of elementary school common a century ago to a stretch of twenty years or more for the child who begins with day care or nursery school and goes on through law or medical school. And even though the age of majority is now eighteen, it's not uncommon for parents to support a child for five or six years into adulthood. During this time, the child will *need* a level of medical care, food, and clothing and will *want* an array of recreational activities and accessories not dreamed of a century ago. Meanwhile, the child's economic contributions to the household may consist of nothing more than once-a-day table setting, twice-a-week trash disposal, or twice-a-month lawn-mowing—often carried out with a less-than-cheerful expression.

Some years before marriage, your child is likely to leave home (often with rent or college costs subsidized by you), and after marriage your financial liability will diminish, but it probably won't end. You may find yourself helping with a down payment on a house, or capitalization of a business venture, or substantial gifts to grandchildren (who presumably constitute additional emotional assets). And your adult children are unlikely to reciprocate beyond the level of birthday and anniversary gifts. Support in your old age will presumably be provided not by your children but by your pension plan and Social Security benefits. In fact, one of your recurring fears may involve the prospect of being dependent on your children—a fear that your children probably share.

This shift of the child from the asset to the liability side of the family ledger may strike you as very depressing. It has, in fact, depressed so many couples that the birth rate of every industrially developed country has dropped sharply. Yet the fact that mature and intelligent couples (and an increasing number of single people) choose to have or adopt children would indicate (1) that a child is, indeed, a very valuable emotional asset and (2) that, although rearing a child is an expensive undertaking, even families with moderate incomes manage it quite successfully. Currently it costs about $100,000 to rear a child from birth to adulthood, but even the family at the median income is likely to earn more than $1 million during its working lifetime. In short, the economic aspects of child-rearing are quite manageable—if you know what you're doing.

COPING WITH THE COSTS

Success in coping with the financial aspects of child-rearing is, oddly enough, not directly related to income. True, very poor parents face severe and often insoluble problems—but many of the very rich make disastrous mistakes. Although there is no simple formula for success, you probably already have at least some of the following characteristics that help parents cope successfully, regardless of their income level.

Awareness of Alternatives   The notion that "information is power" is nowhere more valid than when you make financial plans for your child. For every one of your child's many needs—medical, educational, recreational—there are dozens of alternatives, and you are more likely to miss the best ones because you aren't aware of them than because you can't afford them. Whether it's a choice of a health plan, day-care center, music lessons, summer camp, orthodontist, or college, the more you know, the better off you'll be.

If you think that your neighbor is "dumb" because he keeps his money in a passbook savings account at a low rate of interest and has never heard of the various investments that earn your savings a much higher yield, bear in mind that your neighbor may lose much less through his ignorance than you may by buying the wrong insurance policy or choosing the wrong college.

Foresight   By foresight we don't mean the ability to predict what will happen to the economy or the stock market. (No rational person claims to have this power.) We mean, rather, the tendency to look ahead in order to predict your income and anticipate your expenses and to allow for the possibility of an emergency instead of living one day at a time with a *que será será* attitude. Of course, this foresight comes more easily if your income is stable and your job secure, but many people who have both never acquire it.

Discipline   If you have the discipline to set up a budget and a long-range savings plan of some kind and to resist impulse buying and "once in a lifetime" opportunities that endanger or destroy it, you are likely to come out ahead in terms of both money and peace of mind. This doesn't mean that your plans should be inflexible, that your basic attitude should be one of Scrooge-like self-denial, or that you should never allow yourself and your family a spontaneous, extravagant treat. But it does mean that, within broad limits, your accumulated wealth should keep pace with your rising income.

Autonomy   It's important, too, to feel that you are "*your own person*"—that your sense of personal worth comes from what you *are* and what you *do* rather than what you *own* or what your neighbors think of you. This sense of autonomy can, for example, keep you from overspending on an automobile in order to upstage your neighbors, or sending your child to a private school simply because that's where your boss sends his kids, or taking a vacation in the Caribbean not because you enjoy beaches but because that's where you think the "best" people go. If you can teach your child this same sense of self, the child is likely to be happier—and to cost you less as well.

None of these characteristics is genetically inherited, although you may, of course, have learned them from your parents. But every one of them can be acquired. You may at first feel that this regime for fiscal fitness is just as strenuous and unappetizing as some regimes for physical fitness. But if you carry it out conscientiously you may come to feel, as with a physical fitness program, not only satisfaction with the end result but genuine pleasure in the process itself.

Part I

ACHIEVING FISCAL FITNESS

If all couples were to postpone pregnancy until they were absolutely certain that they could afford a child, the birthrate would fall precipitously close to zero. Very few people are so fortunately situated. And so, even if they've thought carefully about their finances before deciding to have a child, many couples, almost immediately after transmitting the good news of a confirmed pregnancy to their doting parents and in-laws, suffer a sudden anxiety attack about money.

We can't offer you a blanket "everything will be okay" kind of reassurance, but we can point out that the serious financial difficulties people encounter during the early years of parenthood usually stem less from a shortage of money than from a failure to anticipate certain future contingencies. Some of these future events—such as a reduction in the mother's income or an increase in your medical bills—are almost inevitable; others—such as the serious illness or the death of one or both parents—are highly improbable. But all of them are likely to be more manageable if, having anticipated them, you have either prepared for them or protected yourself against them. It's when they take you by surprise that they can be catastrophic.

REDUCTIONS IN INCOME

Most of the countries of western Europe require an employer to provide women with paid maternity leave, and some of them even give fathers paternity leave to help their spouses cope with the arrival of a newborn baby. The United States, in contrast, lags far behind, but some federal laws offer some pregnant women at least a degree of protection.

The Pregnancy Discrimination Act requires that employers of 15 or more employees must treat "women affected by pregnancy, childbirth or related conditions . . . the same for all employment-related purposes . . . as other personnel who are not pregnant but are similar in their ability or inability to work." This means that

> employers cannot require maternity leave of a certain length that bears no relation to the woman's ability or inability to work; employers must reinstate those returning from maternity leave to the same or an equivalent job, benefits, and seniority, and employers must offer leaves of absence for pregnancy and childbirth-related "disabilities" on the same terms they offer employees with other "disabilities."

The Family and Medical Leave Act (FMLA), enacted by Congress in 1993, provides up to 12 weeks of unpaid leave each year for the birth or adoption of a child or to care for a spouse, parent, or child with a serious health condition. In such situations the employer must allow the employee to take the leave and to return to the same or a similar position. And during the leave the employer must continue to make the same benefit contributions, such as health insurance premiums, as the employee was receiving prior to going on leave. However, seniority and pension benefits need not accrue during this leave.

The FMLA applies only to private and public employers with 50 or more employees—only approximately 50% of the work force. And to be eligible the employee must have worked for the employer for at least 1,250 hours and at least one year during the period preceding the leave.

Most couples anticipate this interruption of earnings and budget for it, but often they are a bit optimistic about its duration. According to the U.S. Bureau of Labor Statistics, the average "time out" taken by women for delivery and infant care is six to eight weeks, but if either the mother or the infant develops any kind of complication—if, for example, the infant is premature enough to require special care (as 9% are), or if the mother develops post-partum depression lasting more than a few days or some other pregnancy-related problem (as 25 to 33% do)—this average period becomes meaningless. In such situations, the budget based on normal expectations may need to be supplemented from other sources—preferably from the nest egg we discuss in Chapter 2.

INCREASES IN OUTGO

Even if the "time out" period is about normal and the mother resumes her job as scheduled, the costs of infant care during the parents' working hours can take a substantial bite out of the budget. In some situations a mother or mother-in-law may volunteer to take on the job as an unpaid volunteer, but this kind of help can hardly be expected to continue until the child is old enough for a day-care center or kindergarten. In other situations, one or both parents may be able to arrange a work schedule flexible enough to permit continuous care. But this kind of arrangement can be very stressful if it continues for any length of time.

As we shall see in Chapter 4, good, professional day-care facilities are very scarce, and those that accept infants are even scarcer and more expensive. And so, if one parent holds a full-time job only to earn income and not for the sake of professional satisfaction, he or she might consider "retiring" from full-time employment—at least until the child is ready for kindergarten or old enough to meet the age limit of the typical day-care center.

When the feminist movement was at its height, the role of mother and housewife was rather strongly devalued (although the role of househusband was correspondingly overprized). As a consequence, many young mothers felt it their duty to deny themselves the pleasures of staying home and watching their infants develop and, instead, marched into the labor market to prove themselves equal to their husbands. Today a more rational view prevails, and most people would agree that it makes little sense for a parent to work at a boring or uncongenial job only to spend most or all of the after-tax earnings on a less-than-satisfactory day-care arrangement.

PROTECTING YOUR HEALTH
AND YOUR INCOME

We have had to be frustratingly vague about income reduction and day care, because the situation of every parent is unique in terms of work, family resources, and available professional facilities. But we can be much more specific with respect to protection against excessive medical costs and the loss of income resulting from long-term illness or death. During both pregnancy and the early years of childhood your use of medical services will be higher than they are likely to be for the next forty years, and hence you need to arrange for health insurance coverage or scrutinize very carefully any existing coverage. If possible, this should be done before conception, because some policies pay nothing for prenatal or obstetrical care until they have been in force for at least one year. But if you are not fully covered at the time of conception, the nine months of pregnancy give you ample time to do the research necessary to find the most comprehensive coverage. Chapter 1 will offer you some guidelines.

Whether or not you have health insurance, the fact of conception should start you on a search for good prenatal and obstetrical care. The question of how much prenatal care is necessary is hard to answer. There is no question that women who get little or no prenatal care are more likely to give birth to stillborn, premature, or handicapped infants, but whether these problems are caused by a lack of prenatal care or by the genetic make-up, the malnutrition, the poor health, or the age of women who don't get prenatal care is an open question. In any case, it is better to be safe than sorry and, as we shall see in Chapter 1, a reputable health maintenance organization may offer you maximum protection at a reasonable price.

Your life insurance coverage also needs careful review at this time. The major breadwinner—usually the husband—must, of course, protect the income of his dependents should he die, but the spouse with the major responsibility for child care—usually the mother—should also be covered, because, if she dies, her services may have to be taken over by a paid professional. Although the amount of coverage you'll need for such protection may strike you as beyond your means, you can reduce the cost substantially by buying the most appropriate policies. Chapter 1 suggests ways of getting the best value for your insurance premiums.

Although you may already have some kind of "nest egg" in the form of bank accounts, securities, real estate, or other assets, the fact that you expect a child should motivate you not only to increase its value but also to reconsider your investment strategy and the form of ownership in which the assets are held. Chapter 2 is intended to simplify this often intimidating subject.

Your life and health insurance and your investments have probably concerned you long before your child was born, and her or his birth may merely have prompted you to review and revise them. But once the child has arrived on the scene, you are faced with some new issues. You need to designate a guardian for the child in the unlikely yet possible event that you and your spouse are killed simultaneously in an accident. And, since your child is likely to receive gifts of cash on his birth and on subsequent birthdays, you need to know how to handle these gifts without your incurring tax liability for what is, in fact, the child's money. These are the topics to which we've devoted Chapter 3.

CHAPTER 1

INSURING YOUR LIFE AND YOUR HEALTH

No matter what your income level, you are likely to survive financially unless your income is interrupted by your unemployment or death or your savings are wiped out by a major illness in the family. No private insurance company is reckless enough to offer a policy that protects you against unemployment (and the unemployment insurance provided by the government is both inadequate and temporary), but policies are, of course, available to protect your survivors should you die and to help you with the sometimes catastrophic costs of illness.

Whether or not you can afford adequate coverage depends on the fringe benefits your employer provides, the availability of group insurance through a credit union or other association, your personal health status, and, to some extent, the laws of your state that regulate insurance. But since most life insurance is marketed to individuals by private profit-making companies, you are likely to encounter as much hype and flimflam from insurance salesmen as you are from their counterparts who sell encyclopedias door-to-door. Your best protection against them is a clear understanding of what you want to buy—which may be quite different from what the insurance company would prefer to sell you.

LIFE INSURANCE

A life insurance policy is nothing more than a form of legalized gambling. The insurance company bets that you're not going to die within the next year. You bet, using your premium as the stake, that you will. If you die, you "win" the bet and the insurance company pays off to your beneficiaries. If you don't, the insurance company keeps your premium and you renew the bet by putting up next year's premium.

What are the odds the insurance company uses to set your premiums? Actuarial tables predicting death rates and life expectancies are so accurate that these odds—like the odds in a game of craps or Blackjack—are very precisely known. But if the insurance company were to base its bet with you on these odds, it would actually lose money, since it would pay out as benefits precisely what it took in as premiums and get nothing for its administrative costs or its stockholders. Hence the company, like the Las Vegas gambling casinos, must offer you odds that are somewhat more favorable to itself than the true odds.

This margin in favor of "the house" will vary from one company to another because some may be more administratively efficient than others. But no insurance company is satisfied with the profit that this margin provides. Instead, since they accumulate your premiums until you die, they invest this vast amount of cash in all sorts of financial ventures—mortgages, real estate, money markets, and other investments. And, since it is these ventures that provide the bulk of the profits, they are eager to collect from you just as high a premium as possible by offering you all sorts of expensive, "bells and whistles" policies that go beyond the basic function of protecting your survivors.

The question you need to answer, then, is whether these extras really work to your advantage or whether the higher premiums do nothing more than provide the company with investment capital at your expense. The answer is not the same for everyone, but you may be able to make a sound decision by reviewing the alternatives described later in this chapter.

How Much Is Enough?

Because the basic purpose of life insurance is to protect your survivors against the loss of your income, the amount of coverage you need depends entirely on your personal situation and will change at various stages of your life. At any given time, the proceeds of your policies should, when added to your other assets, allow your spouse and children to maintain the standard of living they now have, but translating this into dollars requires careful thought and calculation.

One commonly used rule of thumb suggests that your coverage should equal three to six times your annual income, but this formula is so broad as to be almost useless. The coverage you need depends on the current and future earnings of your spouse, the ages and the educational needs of your children, income you may be receiving from other investments, the maturity of your home mortgage, your other assets, and your estimate of what your survivors' costs of living are likely to be until your children begin supporting themselves.

A careful calculation along these lines will lead you to two conclusions. The first is that the amount of coverage you need won't remain constant for the next thirty or forty years. If, at the moment, your youngest child will be dependent on you for the next eighteen years or so, if your mortgage payments will go on for perhaps twenty years, and if your spouse's income earning potential is low, you'll probably need enough coverage to provide your survivors with 60 to 75% of your current after-tax income. But twenty years from now, with your children self-sufficient, your mortgage paid off, and your accumulated assets worth more than the face value of your policy, you may need only 40%. From this point of view, the best policy is one that permits you to lower your coverage as time goes on.

On the other hand, there is the problem of inflation. During World War II, the government offered members of the armed forces a life insurance policy with a maximum face value of $10,000 at very low cost. There were few takers for the maximum because it represented, at the time, about five times the average annual income.

Today, of course, this face value provides survivors with less than one year of income, at substantially below the poverty level. The question is, then, whether you can calculate a fixed-dollar coverage that will be eroded by inflation at more or less the same rate as your need for coverage diminishes. Since the inflation rate is entirely unpredictable, and your personal situation is not entirely predictable, the best plan may be to choose a policy or policies that allow you maximum flexibility—a subject to which we'll return shortly.

Where to Buy

Insurance salesmen, no matter how well qualified, work on a commission basis and continue to receive commissions on your policy as long as you continue to pay premiums. Obviously, then, they are interested in selling you as expensive a policy as they can persuade you to buy.

Representatives of a single company will, of course, favor the company's product even though a competing policy may be more suitable, but even independent agents, who sell policies for a number of companies, are motivated by the size of their commissions. Ultimately, you will probably buy at least some insurance through an agent, but you will be far better off if you do your own research and ask him for a premium quotation on the precise type and amount of coverage you've chosen rather than soliciting and following his advice. Even if the agent insists on advising you, the more you've learned about insurance and the more pointed your questions, the less likely you are to be misled. In recent years the insurance commissioners of several states have charged some agents of highly reputable companies with deliberately misleading prospective clients.

Eliminating the services of an agent can reduce your premium costs substantially, and this is possible in two ways. In some states—notably New York—savings banks sell life insurance direct to the buyer, at rates so low that private insurance companies have lobbied strenuously to limit the amount of coverage the banks are allowed to sell. A bank policy is not likely to offer you enough coverage, but making such a policy a part of your coverage can save you money.

A second possibility, more widely available, is the group policy—available through employers, credit unions, professional associations, and fraternal organizations. The group premiums are low because the policies are negotiated directly with the insurer and because administrative costs are low. Moreover, the policies are generally sound because they have been reviewed by experts, and many of them do not require a medical examination. But they have a couple of disadvantages. Your coverage under an employer-sponsored policy may terminate if you leave your job—or the insurer may cancel the group policy and leave you without coverage. Nevertheless, although you may want to consider a group policy only as a supplement to other policies, it is likely to offer the highest level of coverage for the lowest premium—an advantage especially important for young parents.

Types of Policy

What makes buying an insurance policy extremely confusing is the enormous variety of types available as well as the wide variation in premium costs for each type. Our descriptions of the basic types will be followed by suggestions for comparing costs within each type.

Term Insurance Although it is by far the best buy for many young parents, an agent is likely to tell you little or nothing about term insurance—or, indeed, may argue strongly against it—because its low premiums earn him only a scanty commission. Term insurance is a no-frills policy that provides you with protection and nothing but protection. Your premiums buy nothing more than the promise that the policy will pay its face value should you die during its term. Unlike other policies, it is not an investment; it pays no dividends; it accumulates no cash value; you cannot borrow money against it; and it becomes worthless either when you stop paying premiums or at the end of its term. All this may strike you as unattractive, but if you are interested in getting the highest coverage for the lowest premiums, the term policy is unmatchable.

The term of such a policy ranges from five to twenty years, and the premium remains fixed for the duration of the term. The more desirable term policies are renewable term after term without medical examination, although the premium will escalate at each renewal. Thus, if you buy a twenty-year term policy, your premiums remain fixed; if you buy a five-year term your premiums will rise each time you renew it, but you have the option of decreasing your coverage in the later years. In addition, some term policies carry the privilege of conversion to whole-life policies at the expiration of each term.

Another type of term policy—especially desirable if your mortgage is currently high—is known as "decreasing term." Such a policy offers, for a constant but attractively low premium, a high initial face value which decreases steadily for twenty or thirty years as your mortgage decreases or as your other assets accumulate sufficiently to make insurance coverage less essential. Yet another type, the "increasing term" policy, on the other hand, provides for rising amounts of coverage to protect your survivors against inflation.

For most parents, term policies are probably the best buy for all, or at least most, of their life insurance coverage—not only because they provide the highest coverage at the lowest cost but also because they are flexible with respect to coverage.

Whole Life Policies Unlike the term policy, whole-life policies—also called ordinary life, straight life, or cash value policies—require premium payments which remain fixed for your entire lifetime and are based on the age at which you buy the policy. If you buy such a policy at an early age, your premiums will be somewhat higher than for a term policy for the first few years but lower than the premiums you'll pay when you renew the term policy later on.

Whole-life policies combine protection with investment. That is, part of your premium buys protection but part of it buys a continuously increasing "cash value." This cash value may, in some cases, pay periodic dividends—or it can be used to pay future premiums if you develop cash-flow problems, or it can be borrowed against, usually at a favorable interest rate, or it can be transferred to you if you decide to terminate the policy by "cashing it in." If you borrow against your cash value, you need not repay the loan as long as you continue with interest payments, because the insurance company can always deduct the principal from the face value of the policy at the time of your death.

The whole-life policy has a close relative with similar features. The "limited payment," or "20-year payment" policy requires premium payments for a fixed number of years (typically 20 or 30) or until a certain age (typically 65), after which it remains in force without further payments. Obviously the premiums for such a policy will be higher than for the straight-life policy, and you will be paying them early in life when your income is likely to be lower than it will be when you no longer need to pay them.

Whether a whole-life policy strikes you as preferable to term insurance depends to a large extent on your self-discipline in saving money and on your interest and skill in investing it. Because whole-life policies earn them higher commissions, insurance salesmen are likely to stress the advantages of dividends or the steady, tax-free growth in cash value as a result of the company's investments. But independent analysts argue that insurance companies are extremely frugal with dividends, and most of them are rather conservative in making investments. (On the other hand, some insurance companies, having made bad high-risk investments in search of substantial profits, have gone bankrupt, leaving their clients without coverage.) As a consequence, you are likely to fare no better if you buy the whole-life policy in the hope of a return than if you were to buy the cheaper term policy and periodically invest the premium difference yourself.

The more expensive whole-life policy is preferable only as a form of "forced savings"—for people who will pay the monthly premium regularly under threat of cancellation but who lack the discipline to invest a surplus each month when there is no threat involved. But the long-run cost of this attitude can be high—not only because the yield from the policy may be lower than they could earn through do-it-yourself investment of the premium difference but because the higher premium is likely to force them to buy less coverage than they need.

Endowment Policies Like a term insurance policy, the endowment policy offers you protection for a specified period—ten or twenty years, for example, or until age 65. Should you die during this term, your survivors will be paid the full face value. But unlike the term policy, it pays *you* its face value when it terminates—either in a lump sum or in installments. If you anticipate, fifteen years from now, a substantial outlay for college tuition for one of your children, you could schedule an endowment to mature when you need the money. But endowment premiums are high, because they must pay for your life insurance as well as for the endowment, and many independent experts believe that if you were to buy a term policy at far lower cost and use the premium difference for investments of your own choosing, you might not only achieve as good a result but you would be able to use the accumulation at any time instead of having it locked up until the policy matured.

Family Income Policies Adopting some of the features of the decreasing term policy, the level-premium family income policy insures the life of the major breadwinner for his entire life but adds an income supplement for a specified number of years. Thus, for example, on a policy with a face value of $100,000, the income supplement might be 1% or $1,000 a month if the policyholder should die within fifteen years. After the fifteenth year the supplement is no longer payable but the face value continues until death.

Other Types In recent years a number of companies have devised policies that stress their investment function at least as much as their basic function of providing income protection through life insurance. These policies, described as "universal life insurance" or "variable life insurance," offer a wide range of options that are intended to make their premium payments and their face value more flexible and to increase their "cash value" in one way or another. The brochures that describe them, however, relegate to the small print such matters as administrative charges, load charges for each premium payment, and surrender charges. More important, there is no guarantee of a specified return—or that your entire investment may not drop in value, in which case your survivors would get less than you had hoped.

Here, again, you need to decide whether you prefer to hand over most or all of your investment decisions to someone else and, if you do, whether an insurance company is your best choice. An alternative might be to budget life insurance as a separate item, buy maximum coverage through term insurance, and invest whatever surplus you have in ways described in Chapter 2.

COMPARATIVE COSTS AND SURRENDER VALUES OF VARIOUS TYPES OF $100,000 LIFE INSURANCE POLICIES FOR A 35-YEAR-OLD MALE (FEMALE) NONSMOKER IN THE "BEST HEALTH" CATEGORY

Annual Premium	Term[1]	Whole Life[2]	Universal[3]
At age 35	$203 ($182)	$1,152 ($1,000)	$565 ($471)
At age 40	$203 ($182)	$1,152 ($1,000)	$565 ($471)
At age 45	$203 ($182)	$1,152 ($1,000)	$565 ($471)
At age 50	$203 ($182)	$1,152 ($1,000)	$565 ($471)
At age 55	$803 ($534)	$1,152 ($1,000)	$565 ($471)

Surrender Value			
In 5 years	0	$3,893 ($3,477)[4]	$1,383 ($1,113)[5]
In 10 years	0	$12,222 ($10,605)	$4,793 ($3,747)
In 15 years	0	$23,199 ($20,105)	$9,046 ($7,060)
In 20 years	0	$37,063 ($32,197)	$13,705 ($10,769)

Source: Continental Assurance Co.

[1]This term policy is renewable every 20 years. Premiums are higher for applicants who cannot pass medical examinations.
[2]Premiums on whole life policies remain level.
[3]Premiums on universal policies are flexible.
[4]Surrender value on the whole life policy will vary with interest rates. A 6% interest rate is shown; guaranteed rates are lower.
[5]Surrender values on the universal life policy will vary with premiums and interest rates. A 6% interest rate is shown; guaranteed rates are lower.

Who Should NOT Be Covered

Once they have sold you as much coverage as you can possibly afford, ambitious insurance agents are likely to try selling you policies for other members of your family. These should be scrutinized skeptically. Your spouse should be covered sufficiently to compensate for her earnings if she is employed or to replace her with paid help if she is a homemaker and the mother of young children. Insuring the children makes no sense at all, because they earn no income, because the death rate in children beyond the age of one is very low, and because money would not compensate you in the highly improbable event that your child should die before you.

Sources of Information

As we have noted, insurance agents, regardless of their qualifications, are likely to be both overeager to earn commissions and biased toward certain products. If, however, you need to use an agent, select one who is entitled to use the letters C.L.U. (Chartered Life Underwriter) after his name. This indicates that he has passed a fairly rigorous examination, is reasonably well informed, and has demonstrated some degree of professionalism. He may be biased, but he is less likely to mislead you deliberately—especially if you are prepared to ask knowledgeable questions.

Consumer Reports periodically publishes sophisticated and unbiased evaluations of insurance policies which may help you select not only the best policy type but also the most reliable company. *Best's Insurance Reports,* available at many public libraries, periodically rates individual companies on the basis of financial stability.

If it is aggressively consumer-oriented, your state insurance commission may be a useful source of information, since it regulates the industry within your state and handles consumer complaints. In addition, some states publish detailed evaluations of companies and policies, and these can be extremely useful to consult before making a final decision. In general, no matter how attractive its premiums or its policy, it is unwise to buy insurance from a company not authorized to do business within your state—or from one about which the state commission has had a significant number of complaints.

Comparing Policy Costs

Comparing the actual costs of two policies of the same type on the basis of their premiums can be very difficult, because the true costs may be distorted by differences in the premium schedules, dividend payments, the accrual of cash value, and other factors difficult to identify or calculate.

Fortunately, many states now require insurers to present to the potential customer, along with each policy, a figure known as the "interest-adjusted cost index" together with instructions for using it. Although this index may sometimes be preceded by a dollar sign, it is not a premium figure but simply an index that provides for an accurate comparison of two seemingly identical policies. In connection with term policies, for example, indexes are available for five-, ten-, and twenty-year terms. Other things being equal, the policy with the lower index is the less expensive one.

Cost comparisons between whole life policies require the use of two cost indexes. The "net cost" or "surrender" index reflects the cost if you hold the policy for a specified number of years and then surrender it for its cash value. The "net payment" index reflects the cost if you hold the policy until you die without cashing it in. In comparing two or more policies, both indexes should be used because they may not be consistent for each policy.

Although these indexes are very useful, bear in mind that a small index difference between two policies may not be significant and may be offset by differences in the financial strength of the company, the services promised by the agent, or small differences in service features of the policies themselves.

Designating Your Beneficiaries

If you are buying your own policy, your application will not be processed until you have designated the policy's beneficiaries. But if you get coverage as part of your fringe benefits, your employer's personnel department may neglect to ask you to specify the beneficiaries or to record your designation. If the policy is to benefit the persons you have chosen, the beneficiaries must not only be specified but must be kept up to date as your family situation changes—when, for example, a child reaches the age of majority.

Your choice of beneficiaries will depend on whether you are married or single and whether your children are minors or adults. Most parents designate their spouse as primary beneficiary and their children as alternates but, as we shall see in Chapter 11, setting up a trust and designating its trustee as the sole beneficiary may be a sounder arrangement.

HEALTH INSURANCE

If yours is a typical middle-income family, the actual costs of medical and dental care will absorb a substantial part of your income. And, because the cost of these services has been escalating more rapidly than the Consumer Price Index, they may well take a larger bite out of your budget in the years to come—assuming that you don't suffer a catastrophic illness that wipes you out financially. Small wonder, then, that some form of health insurance, paid for in whole or in part by employers, is widely regarded as the most attractive of a range of fringe benefits. It currently covers 60% of the U.S. population and will, in the near future, cover an increasing percentage of the population.

If your employer provides health insurance as part of your fringe benefits, you may be captive to the policy it includes—but you may be a fairly contented captive. These group policies, if they are efficiently marketed and administered and if they have been negotiated to provide optimal benefits, are usually a better bargain than any policy you could buy as an individual.

If you are self-employed, or if your employer does not provide you with coverage, you can participate as an individual in a number of the plans described below, but these are worth reviewing even if health insurance is part of your employment benefits package. For one thing, many large employers offer an option of two or more plans, and understanding the alternatives can help you make a sound choice. For another, a clear understanding of the differences between plans may either reduce your dissatisfaction with what you are offered or motivate you to suggest a better plan to your employer.

Fee-for-Service Plans

Fee-for-service plans either permit you to choose your own physician or select one from a list of preferred providers, who charge fees that are normally paid in full by the insurer. If you choose a physician not on the list, the insurer will pay what it regards as a "reasonable" fee, leaving any excess to be paid out of your pocket.

Although they permit you to choose any licensed *physician,* most plans exclude the services of dentists, optometrists, and chiropractors, and many place limits on reimbursement for psychotherapy or other psychological treatment. And some of them won't pay for what they consider "elective" surgery. That is, they will pay for removal of a gall bladder but not for a face lift. Some of them provide no reimbursement for prescription drugs; others require a stipulated co-payment from the patient. Although they allow you to choose your own physician (which, as we shall note shortly, may or may not be an advantage), these plans can turn out to be expensive if your physician consistently charges you more than the "reasonable" reimbursement you get from the insurer.

But regardless of whether or not they satisfy their participants, almost all fee-for-service plans are becoming increasingly expensive for employers—for an obvious reason: since the physician can bill the insurer for each and every test or laboratory procedure he orders, he may well prescribe a number of them that benefit his cash flow more than they benefit the patient. Although some health-insurers monitor what physicians do, many take a laissez-faire approach and pass the higher costs on to the employer in the form of higher premiums. This is why, in recent years, employers have been eagerly seeking less expensive alternatives, some of which may strike you as less satisfactory than the traditional methods of selecting and paying physicians.

Health Maintenance Organizations

An increasingly popular alternative to the fee-for-service plan is membership (employer-provided or individual) in a health maintenance organization (HMO). Some HMOs are operated by nonprofit organizations, others by private-sector corporations, but all of them function on more or less the same principles.

Under the HMO plan, your employer or you pay a fixed annual premium, in return for which you receive *all* health services, including routine examinations, surgery, hospitalization, and all necessary laboratory tests, at no additional cost, although there may be a nominal co-payment for prescription drugs. The larger HMOs (such as Kaiser Permanente) maintain their own medical centers and in some locations even a hospital, and treatment is provided by a salaried group of general practitioners and specialists. Smaller HMOs use a local hospital and a panel of what are called Preferred Providers—community physicians who bill the HMO at reduced rates for services to its clients.

Employers generally favor HMOs because they cost less than fee-for-service plans, but many employees are less enthusiastic, especially before they or their dependents have undergone any treatment. For one thing, they worry about the quality of the treatment that the HMO is likely to provide. And their concern is reasonable. After all, if fee-for-service physicians are tempted to provide too much in the way of treatment in order to increase their incomes, isn't it likely that HMO physicians will cut corners and undertreat their patients in order to lower the organization's costs and thus undercut the competition? And isn't this especially likely when HMOs are operated by profit-making corporations who are obligated to worry about the bottom line?

Although HMOs are too numerous to permit any firm generalizations about their quality of care, careful comparative studies done on a number of well-established HMOs conclude that the treatment they provide is at least as good as—and in some cases considerably better than—that provided by physicians practicing under a fee-for-service arrangement. True, HMO patients undergo less frequent hospitalization and remain in hospital for shorter stays, but the HMOs argue that the reduction in the number of hospitalizations is the result of their active program of preventive medicine and that many longer hospital stays benefit the hospital and the physician rather than the patient. Studies of the health status of HMO patients generally confirm that the HMOs are doing a good job. Moreover, because the single annual premium covers all costs, no matter how much service participants use, they are likely to consult a physician promptly instead of neglecting what may turn out to be a serious illness.

Another feature that makes some people hesitate to enroll is that most HMOs do not permit patients to choose their own physician but assign them, instead, to one of the members of the HMO staff. But whether this restriction really matters is open to question. If you think about it honestly, you may admit that you have very little basis for judging the professional competence of your current physician and, hence, that you've probably chosen him or her on the basis of hearsay, personality, "bedside manner," ethnic background, age, or some other largely irrelevant characteristic. The HMOs, on the other hand, are more likely to use more rational criteria for assessing the competence of the physicians they hire, and these organizations monitor physicians' performance continuously. And if you've ever had a health problem that was serious or critical, you were very happy to abandon these criteria and entrust the choice of a specialist to your general practitioner, knowing that he would base his choice on professional rather than personal qualifications.

Many patients do, of course, feel somewhat uncomfortable at the prospect of confronting an unfamiliar physician, especially if they encounter a new face on each of their visits to the HMO. But this is unlikely to be the case, because patients are assigned to HMO physicians on a long-term basis. In any case, good medical treatment depends less on a physician's personal familiarity with you than on meticulous record-keeping and on the quality and training of the medical staff. If your medical record is sufficiently clear and detailed, any conscientious and well-trained physician is likely to prescribe the most appropriate treatment, even though he has never laid eyes on you before. Moreover, if it turns out that you're dissatisfied with the physician to whom you've been assigned, most HMOs of any size will offer you another choice.

The fact that the HMO, because of its efficiency, is likely to cost your employer less may be of no consequence to you. But HMO membership may have distinct advantages for you and your children. To begin with, the emphasis on preventive medicine may reduce the number and severity of your own family's illnesses and the frequency and length of its hospitalizations, as it has for other HMO patients. And, because it serves a large patient population, an HMO can afford to have at hand many more resources than a doctor in private or group practice. This is why a high-quality HMO can provide not only ready access to a wide range of specialists who serve either as staff members or as consultants but also 24-hour emergency service. And, because children often choose the middle of the night to develop alarming symptoms, this is no small advantage.

There are, however, a couple of possible disadvantages. If the HMO operates its own office facilities, their proximity to your home may be an important consideration. And, although some HMOs will reimburse patients who, in the course of vacations or business trips, need treatment by out-of-town physicians, others will not.

Making a Choice

If your employer-paid health insurance plan is provided on a take-it-or-leave-it basis, there is little you can do about it. If it's a fee-for-service plan, you can, of course, continue to use your current physician and simply take advantage of whatever reimbursement the plan provides. If it's an HMO—and the trend is strongly in this direction—you can choose to ignore its benefits and continue paying your own physician out of your own pocket, but you would be wiser to set aside whatever reservations you may have and try it out—especially for such routine matters as well-baby check-ups and childhood immunizations.

The current status of your family, as well as its health history, can also offer you some guidance. You can take it for granted that pregnancy, infancy, and the very early childhood years involve a good deal of medical attention—for prenatal care, well-baby check-ups, the to-be-expected ear infections and gastric upsets, and other routine, nonemergency procedures. But a child's middle years are likely to be very healthy, with only an occasional playground injury requiring a doctor's care.

Your own health also needs review. It is possible that, aside from an annual check-up (the usefulness of which is being increasingly questioned), you and your spouse need very little medical care. On the other hand, if either of you suffers from any kind of chronic problem that needs monitoring—recurring ovarian cysts, for example, or a skin condition that requires periodic treatment, or high blood pressure—your medical costs may be considerable. Although medical catastrophes—heart attacks, automobile accidents, and the onset of cancer—can't be foretold, these are fairly improbable in adults before middle age, and the psychologist's axiom that the best predictor of future performance is recent past performance applies to health as well as to other areas.

A Policy of Your Own

Until recently, people who lost their jobs, or divorced a spouse who was covered by health insurance, or came of age and thus were no longer covered by a parent's policy, suddenly found themselves without health insurance. But today federal law requires insurers to allow you to continue your group coverage for more than a year—sufficient time to allow you to shop around for an individual policy. Under this law, you pay the employer's share of the premium plus your own share (if any) plus a 2% surcharge, but this sum is still substantially less than you are likely to pay for an individual policy.

On the other hand, if you are self-employed or if your employer does not provide coverage and you can find none through an association of some sort, you may want to buy an individual policy to cover yourself and your family. This is certain to cost more than a group policy (because administrative costs are higher) and it may offer less coverage (because the terms of the policy will not have been negotiated by a sophisticated representative of the employer). In addition, it is all too easy to be misled by the promises of insurance companies that use extensive television and media advertising to sell individual policies to unsophisticated individuals. Your best protection against disappointment or unpleasant surprises is to know exactly what type of coverage you need and what kind of "small print" exclusions to look out for. In this connection your state insurance commissioner may be a useful source of help.

Types of Coverage

Unlike the HMO, which serves almost all of its members' health needs for one annual fee, most health insurance policies limit their coverages rather narrowly and surround them with numerous exclusions. A review of the most common coverages may help you to choose the type of policy most appropriate for you—or lead you to conclude that an HMO is your best choice.

Hospitalization This policy covers most, if not all, of the charges you will incur when you are hospitalized: semiprivate room charges, laboratory tests, X-ray procedures, radiation therapy, and so forth. But it does *not* cover hospitalization for cosmetic surgery, and it may not cover surgery performed on an out-patient basis, the fees charged by the surgeon or the anesthetist, obstetrical services provided less than nine months after the coverage is in effect, and any other bills for a physician's services.

A number of private insurers offer mail-order hospitalization policies, but you need to scrutinize these carefully. Typically, they provide a specified per diem amount or a specified maximum for hospitalization, which is almost always insufficient to cover the entire bill, and they contain numerous exclusions and exceptions. Some, for example, do not pay for the first several days of hospitalization—a period that may exceed your actual stay. Some, although they require no medical examination, have numerous exclusions for preexisting conditions. Some promise payment over and above the patient's reimbursement from other policies, but most medical insurers prohibit such duplication. More important, these companies disallow a significantly higher proportion of claims than other insurers. Before dealing with any mail-order insurance company, check with your state insurance commissioner to make certain the company is licensed in your state and does not have a disproportionate number of complaints filed against it.

Medical-Surgical Medical-surgical policies cover physicians' and surgeons' charges—usually in connection with hospitalization but in some cases including office visits. They may or may not cover the outpatient therapeutic services often required after surgery. Whether this kind of policy will cover all your costs depends on whether your physician and surgeon are willing to accept payment based on the insurer's scale of "reasonable" charges for specific procedures. If they are not, you remain responsible for the balance.

Major Medical A major medical policy is designed not to cover all your costs but to protect you from the impact of very high medical bills in the course of a year. Thus, most such policies have an annual deductible for each member of your family, ranging from $100 to $1,000, depending on the premium. Once you have paid the deductible, the insurer will copay a proportion of the balance—typically 75 to 80%. Most such policies have a stop-loss clause. Thus, for example, if in the course of a year your share of your medical costs amounts to as much as $1,500, the copayment ceases and the insurer pays 100% of the balance. On the other hand, although some policies set no lifetime limits on benefits, others specify maximums ranging from $100,000 to $1,500,000.

Although these policies contain some exclusions—typically, for routine ophthalmology services, dental work, long-term treatment of mental illness, and elective surgery—they offer far broader coverage than the medical-surgical policies. Many of them cover drugs, private nursing, prosthetic devices, and post-surgery rehabilitation. Most exclude routine medical check-ups, but some physicians evade this restriction by classifying such visits as follow-ups intended to monitor a specific chronic condition.

Other Coverages Policies that provide partial or total reimbursement for dental and optometric services are desirable components of a fringe benefits package but are of questionable value if you have to pay the premium yourself unless you or your family members have a history of dental or vision problems. Many such policies base reimbursement on a scale of "reasonable" charges which often seem more reasonable to the insurer than to the physician who bills you.

Disability policies—which protect you against income loss in case of illness or accident—should be bought from private insurers only in exceptional circumstances. In many cases, your employer's policy on sick leave or the state worker's compensation system (if your illness or injury is job-related) may offer you equivalent protection at no direct cost to you. If you consider buying such a policy, read its terms with suspicion, because many of these policies contain even more exclusions than mail-order hospitalization policies, and they illustrate their benefits with carefully selected "true" histories of cases that are highly improbable.

Some Alternatives

Although a catastrophic illness or injury that wipes out your savings and ends your income is always a possibility, it's important to recognize that it is not very likely. Hence, the lack of insurance coverage should not panic you. But it should motivate you, before the need arises, to shop around in your community for trustworthy and inexpensive medical and dental care instead of relying on the emergency room at the local hospital, which will probably turn out to be your most costly option.

One source of good and relatively inexpensive health care is the "family practice center," which has become increasingly a part of every teaching hospital or medical school. Staffed by young residents interested in family practice, these centers offer most of the services of an HMO but charge a moderate fee for service instead of an annual fee. Contrary to widespread belief, these clinics are intended to serve the entire community, not just the indigent. Treatment is usually very good, because the residents are well trained and carefully supervised.

In addition, many communities have seen a significant increase in the number of "free standing" (also called "walk-in") clinics—staffed by physicians who find group practice congenial and who are able to charge far less than hospital emergency rooms. Although these clinics do not treat serious illnesses, their no-appointment-necessary policy makes them ideal for the treatment of childhood illnesses, injuries, and minor health problems.

Competent dental work can be obtained—at little or no cost—from students at most dental school clinics. The thought of entrusting a dental student with your fillings or your child's orthodontia may be disconcerting, but the only serious threat is not to your teeth but to your patience. Student dentists work under the most meticulous supervision and this, together with their inexperience, can slow up the process considerably.

CHAPTER 2

NEST EGGS: LAYING, INCUBATING, AND HATCHING THEM

In addition to the day-to-day costs of your child's food, clothing, shelter, and medical care, most of which you take for granted and pay for out of your income, you are probably painfully aware that there could be some "big ticket" items in your child's future: orthodontia, summer camp, perhaps a trip to Europe, a saddle horse, a $3,000 cello or a car, and, inevitably, college. To pay for all these anticipated items—and for some that are not foreseeable—it's a sound idea to build some sort of nest egg to which you can contribute a regular amount each month and perhaps the occasional windfall.

The advantages of this kind of systematic accumulation are several. Once the monthly contributions become part of your regular budget, you're likely to regard them as part of your cost of living and to write the checks as routinely as you do for your home mortgage. If you contribute a fixed sum each month, it's likely to become less burdensome as your income increases over the years—or, if you prefer, you can increase the monthly amount as your income rises. Prudently invested, the nest egg can achieve gratifying growth, especially because, as we shall see, you may be able to reduce or avoid income taxes on its yield and growth.

These advantages are so widely recognized by so many parents that, like diaper-service salesmen, hordes of investment salesmen spend their days monitoring newspaper birth announcements so that they can be on the site when the happy new parents are in a receptive—or perhaps especially vulnerable—frame of mind. But before we concern ourselves with selecting the kinds of investments that might flourish best in your nest egg, we need to deal with some broader issues.

WHOSE NEST EGG IS IT?

Your decisions about what the nest egg should contain—cash, stocks, bonds, or all of the above—can have a powerful effect on its growth. But there is a decision that you need to make even before you start out: Who is going to own the nest egg while it's a-building—you or the child?

Owning It Yourself

Whatever the form of your nest egg—savings account, certificates of deposit, mutual fund, brokerage account, etc.—there is no reason why you can't register it in your own name or in joint tenancy with your spouse and simply make a mental note that this account is "for Susie's college education." Do this and you retain complete control over the assets. You can, for example, "borrow" from them temporarily to prepay or refinance a mortgage, to take advantage of an unexpected bargain, investment, or business opportunity, or for any other purpose that requires a large lump sum on short notice. And if it should turn out that Susie celebrates her seventeenth birthday in a home for delinquent girls instead of a Vassar dorm, you can use the nest egg in ways best designed to console you.

But owning the nest egg yourself has two disadvantages. First, there is the not-always-warranted assumption that you will have the discipline necessary to repay any money you borrow and the acumen not to lose it in an ill-fated business venture. More important, as long as you retain ownership of the nest egg, you retain full responsibility for paying state and federal income taxes on whatever it earns. Holding the nest egg in joint tenancy with your spouse means that you share the tax liability, but this is meaningless if you file a joint return. Moreover, since each joint tenant has full control of the nest egg, the prerequisite for such an arrangement is a very stable marriage.

There are, as we'll see in Chapter 3, two ways of shifting the income tax liability to your lower-bracket child, but these require you to relinquish some control of the nest egg—and all rights to use it for your own purposes.

Are Taxes That Important?

Unless you derive psychic gratification out of depriving the IRS of revenue, your decision about the ownership of the nest egg should not be based on the income-tax consequences alone—at least not until you've calculated them accurately. Assume, for example, that the nest egg yields $1,000 per year. If you are in the 28% bracket, you will pay federal income tax of $280 on the earnings. If, however, you give the nest egg to the child by way of a custodial account, he or she becomes responsible for paying the tax but is entitled to a $600 standard deduction (see p. 55). The income is taxed at the child's rate* and thus the child pays $75. The question you need to ask yourself is whether the tax saving of $214 is worth your relinquishing control over the more than $20,000 needed to generate the $1,200 of income.

But income tax is not your only consideration. If your nest egg takes the form of a custodial account or a trust for minors, and if you contribute to it more than $10,000 in any one year ($20,000 with the consent of your spouse), you will be liable for Federal Gift and Estate Tax (see p. 170).

HOW WILL THE NEST EGG GROW?

Even sophisticated investors who have been quite successful in accumulating assets for themselves can make mistakes in connection with a nest egg for their child if they overlook fundamental differences between their personal investment goals and needs and those of a child. An awareness of these differences can prevent you from simply replicating your own investment tactics, no matter how successful, on behalf of your child.

The Long-Range View

Unlike most of your own assets, which may fluctuate widely and often in response to your spending patterns, your child's nest egg will

---

*If a child under the age of 14 has investment income exceeding $1,200, part of that income will be taxed at the parents' rate.

probably have a relatively long and stable life. If you're lucky—that is, if your child turns out not to need orthodontia or psychotherapy, or if she goes to camp free as a junior counselor, or she gets a full scholarship to a music conservatory—the nest egg may incubate for more than 15 years before you need to hatch it. If she gets a full college scholarship, you can add another four years to its life before it may be needed for graduate school or wedding expenses.

The fact that you're unlikely to need to liquidate all or most of the nest egg on short notice offers you a substantial advantage, because the yield on any investment—whether in terms of interest, dividends, or appreciation—is influenced by its liquidity: that is, the speed with which you can turn it into cash with minimal loss in its value. The higher the liquidity, the lower the yield—and vice versa. This is why five-year certificates of deposit (which carry a penalty for early liquidation) yield a higher interest rate than one-year certificates or than savings accounts (which may be withdrawn at any time). By the same token, many common stocks offer a better rate of return than, say, money-market mutual funds because the latter can be instantaneously liquidated at what you paid for them, whereas the former may have to be sold at a loss if you need the money when their price has dropped. Consequently, since the nest egg is not likely to require liquidation very soon or on short notice, it can earn at a better rate than your personal savings.

But the fact that you are investing the nest egg for the long term also creates a problem, because during its lifetime both interest rates and general economic conditions are almost certain to fluctuate, and hence the yields and the value of any investment are likely to change. And so, locking the entire nest egg into an inflexible investment that has low liquidity may prevent you from taking advantage of new investment opportunities that are bound to occur during this long incubation period.

Long-term Treasury bonds, for example, are regarded as one of the safest possible investments, but if you buy $10,000 worth of them when the prime rate is 7% and the prime rate five years subsequently rises to 10%, nobody will want to buy them from you for more than $7,000, although you will still get back your $10,000 if you hold them to maturity. But whether the $10,000 you get back will buy what it did when you bought the bonds will depend on the rate of inflation. On the other hand, if you put all of the money into a stock portfolio, a mutual fund, or any other investment whose price "moves with the market," its value may be at an all-time low at the very time when you need to liquidate it.

Since nobody can predict fluctuations in either the interest rate or the state of the economy (or the relationship between them), the best policy is to diversify between long-term and short-term investments—that is, between instruments that "lock in" current yields for a long time and those that can be liquidated promptly when conditions change.

The long life of the nest egg also permits you to use "dollar-cost averaging," an investment tactic recommended by many experts. It involves investing a fixed number of dollars each month in, say, a mutual fund or a stock, regardless of the current price of the shares. Since your fixed number of dollars will buy fewer shares when the price is high and more shares when the price is low, the price fluctuations will average out over the long term, and you will have accumulated the shares at a good price.

The Question of Safety

Just as the liquidity of a particular investment affects its yield, so, too, does its safety. In general, the safer an investment—that is, the lower the likelihood that you will lose part or all of your money—the lower its yield. This is why savings accounts (which are insured by the federal government) pay less interest than uninsured money-market mutual funds, and why the bonds of such blue-chip companies as AT&T or Pillsbury yield less than those of some smaller and less established firms. It explains also why blue-chip stocks are less likely to rise sharply than the stock of some aggressive, innovative newcomers. In short, just as you pay a premium for an insurance policy that minimizes losses on your house and your car, so, too, you pay a premium (in the form of lower yields) for protecting your investment against shrinkage or obliteration.

On the other hand, high risk may be highly rewarding. Put $5,000 into IBM and you can be pretty certain that you won't lose most of it and that you won't get rich. Put the same amount into a fledgling company (as IBM was in 1911) and you have a good chance of losing it all but also a chance of becoming very rich indeed.

Your attitude toward risk depends, of course, on your general level of income and your style of budgeting. In connection with your personal savings, you may prefer a rather conservative approach, choosing investments that offer relatively low earnings and little prospect of rapid growth but that can be liquidated quickly with little or no loss should you need a new car or find an irresistible new house. But your child's nest egg, because it is unlikely to be liquidated for many years, is likely to ride out several fluctuations in interest rates and several ups and downs of the economic cycle. Hence, you may be willing to invest it in a combination of instruments, some long-term and some short, some safe and some relatively risky.

What's a "Good" Yield?

Thus far we've been describing the yield that an investment produces as "high" or "low" without attaching any precise figures to these adjectives. But we've had good reasons for this reticence, because there is no way of describing a rate of, say, 6% as low, average, or dangerously high. The only way to assess a rate of return is to subtract from it the most recent annual rate of inflation. Thus, when inflation is running at 1%, a passbook savings rate of 3.25% is not merely low; it's negative, because at the end of a year your account, after you've paid income taxes on its yield, will have less buying power than you started out with. When the inflation rate is 9%, an 11% return will net you 2%, but when the inflation rate drops to 4%, a 6% return will give you the same results.

Of course, your *yield* on common stocks does not indicate your total return, because it includes only the dividends you receive (which may fluctuate unpredictably). Your *total return* on a stock includes not only dividends but also any difference between the price at which you bought it and the price at which you will sell it—and this is also unpredictable.

CAN YOU GET GOOD ADVICE?

No book can label either a type of investment (money market funds, for example, or common stocks) or the stock of a specific company (Quaker Oats, for example) as a "best buy" for all investors. And so, once you've made some general decisions on the basis of the general advice offered above, you will probably want to find an expert to help you place your money where it will best accomplish your aims in terms of safety, liquidity, yield, and growth.

Unfortunately, although many people—financial planners, accountants, insurance salesmen, stock brokers, and others—label themselves as experts, their performance over the long term doesn't justify this label. And this negative evaluation applies not only to the "experts" available to the small investor through local banks and brokerage firms but also to those money managers who handle billion-dollar portfolios for pension funds and other mammoth-scale investors. Although many of them can legitimately boast of above-average performance over the course of a year or two, none has shown consistently superior results over a period that will equal the life expectancy of your child's nest egg.

On the other hand, the individual investor, whether he studies the market very carefully or operates purely by hunch, may not fare any better. It's not uncommon to hear, at cocktail parties, the success stories of individuals who have "made a killing" on the stock market. But individuals who have "taken a bath" on Wall Street may be just as numerous, even though they are less likely to use their experience as material for small talk.

The Professionals

Most states have laws prohibiting a physician from operating a pharmacy on the side. Their purpose is, of course, to discourage the physician from prescribing for his patients unnecessary but profitable drugs. Unfortunately, very few state laws prohibit anyone—financial planners, insurance salesmen, stock brokers, or mutual fund salesmen, for example—from recommending investment instruments to a client and then earning a commission or a profit by selling them. Thus, your local banker is likely to sing the praises of bank instruments—certificates of deposit, for example, or, more recently, bank-sponsored mutual funds—but to tell you little or nothing about stocks and bonds. Similarly, the account executive in a brokerage firm is likely to tout the products he sells—stocks, bonds, options, and futures—and perhaps to recommend with special enthusiasm a stock that his firm has underwritten. But he is likely to tell you nothing about mutual funds that you can buy without commission. Moreover, since he earns a commission on every transaction, he may "churn" your account—that is, buy and sell frequently—at considerable profit to himself but little or none to you.

All this would be of no consequence if you were to find an advisor whose recommendations turned out to be consistently profitable. But, as we've noted, this is altogether unlikely—especially for the small investor. Successful stock-market trading depends not on intelligence or insight or a mastery of economics but on information: information about take-overs, unanticipated profits or losses, and other facts that are highly perishable and not widely publicized. By the time this information makes its way down to the level of the typical account executive, the prices of the stocks involved have already responded to it, and you're simply too late to do anything profitable.

Why is it, then, that some account executives can boast that stocks they have recommended have gone up? There are three possible answers to this question: First, when the research department of a large nationwide brokerage firm recommends a stock, so many of its customers flock to buy it that its price rises—at least temporarily—and the recommendation becomes a self-fulfilling prophecy. Second, the market as a whole may be going up and most, though not all, boats rise with the tide. Third, it may be a matter of luck: since stocks either go up or go down over time, even a totally uninformed prediction is likely to be right half the time. And a moment's thought may lead you to conclude that if an account executive were omniscient about the market, he would be accumulating millions for himself while lying at ease in a poolside lounge chair in Palm Springs and trading in stocks over a WATS line or a fax machine with his own broker instead of eking out a living by selling stocks to small traders like yourself.

Doing It Yourself

If suddenly you were to get a windfall of $25,000, you might well be anxious and uncertain about how and where to invest it, and you'd be eager for help—although the quality of this help might turn out to be no better than what we've just described. But your child's nest egg is unlikely to start out as such an intimidating lump sum. Instead, it will probably have modest beginnings. And so, whether you start out with a passbook savings account or a relatively small certificate of deposit, any mistake you make in investing it will have only negligible consequences.

If, as the nest egg grows, you set to work to learn more about investing, your sophistication is likely to grow faster than the nest egg itself, and very shortly you will find yourself familiar with the investment alternatives open to you and the various ways of growing the nest egg and protecting it against serious losses.

You won't, of course, acquire this understanding by reading the perennial crop of books on how to make a fortune in the stock market or in gold trading. (Anyone familiar with the effort involved in writing a how-to-get-rich book and the relatively low returns it yields will realize that the author would earn far more by practicing than preaching his system if it actually worked.) But there are a number of low-keyed, sensible books that explain investments instead of touting a particular system or formula, and careful study of a number of them can make your investments sensible and relatively safe.

Learning about investing does take time, but it does not require inordinate intelligence. Anyone who can master the rules and statistics that surround football or baseball should have no trouble whatever with the rudiments of the securities market. The knowledge you gain can, of course, be applied to your own investments—even if they consist of nothing more than your IRA—and your growing interest may cause you to turn to the financial section of your morning newspaper before you go to the sports pages.

Of course, stocks and bonds can be traded only through a broker, but the growing number of do-it-yourself investors has led to the development of discount brokerage firms. These "no-frills" brokers offer cut-rate commissions because they have no costly research departments and they provide their customers with no advice. Their account executives, being salaried order takers, have no incentive to churn your account or to urge you to trade actively in order to maximize their commissions, but in most other respects they provide the same services as full-service brokers and they operate all over the country, both through local offices and through toll-free telephone lines. Using such a firm can save you more than 60% of your commission costs every time you buy or sell a stock. This may not seem to amount to much, but over the years you're likely to save a fair amount of money that you would otherwise be paying for services you don't use.

On the other hand, if you simply haven't the time or interest to follow your own investments, you might consider a full-service broker. If you can visit and interview account executives at two or three firms, you may find one who seems personally congenial and quick to grasp your financial situation and your investment aims.

But bear in mind two caveats. First, small investors such as you are assigned to neophyte account executives, who may be personally charming but less competent and experienced than their colleagues who handle the large, active, commission-rich accounts. Second, the only way you have of assessing your account executive's performance is to check on whether your investments keep pace with the Dow Jones or New York Stock Exchange indexes. And the fact that they do is no proof that you would not have done just as well or better by making your own investment decisions.

FILLING THE NEST

Because we assume that, like most parents, you'll be starting out on a small scale rather than with a substantial lump sum, we'll deal first with investment options than can be started with a small amount of money and we'll go on to those that require larger minimums and involve increasing degrees of risk.

Bank Accounts

Although a passbook savings account pays a very low rate of interest, it has its uses. Essentially, it's a convenient depository for small monthly contributions, occasional cash gifts from grandparents, and small dividend and interest checks (from other nest-egg investments) until its balance grows large enough to meet minimum requirements for a higher-yielding investment. Passbook accounts can usually be opened with a minimum deposit of $50 or less, and there is no minimum for additional deposits. Full-service banks tend to pay a lower rate on savings accounts than do savings banks or savings and loan associations, but the additional services that they provide are likely to be unnecessary for your child's nest-egg account.

Banks and other thrift institutions also offer certificates of deposit (CDs), which, like their regular accounts, are federally insured by the FDIC or the FSLIC. The minimum investment, typically, is $500, and the interest rates paid are higher than those for passbook savings accounts and increase with the term of the certificate: that is, 7-year certificates pay a higher rate than 90-day certificates.

All certificates of deposit carry a penalty for liquidation before maturity, but this is a less important concern for a child's nest egg than it might be for your personal funds. On the other hand, tying up a large sum in a single long-term certificate of deposit leaves you at the mercy of rising interest rates, which would make the certificate's fixed yield less attractive. If, then, you plan to invest $5,000 in CDs, the smart way to do it is to buy five $1,000 certificates at six-month or one-year intervals. In this way, some of the money would become available periodically for alternative investments that may become more attractive.

Both banks and thrift institutions compete vigorously for the sale of CDs by offering various rates and other incentives. Although you may find differing rates within your own community, these differences are likely to be even greater between one region of the country and another. The *New York Times* and some financial papers regularly publish not only the rates offered by various banks but also a rating of each bank's financial condition. In addition, Veribanc, Inc. (800-442-2657) provides data on the financial soundness of banks for a fee of $10 for assessing one bank and $5 for each additional one. And Standard and Poor's Corporation (212-208-1527) provides bank credit ratings at no charge. Using these sources, you can feel comfortable about buying a CD by mail.

Money-Market Mutual Funds

A money market fund is similar to a CD in that it maintains your investment in dollars rather than in shares and it pays a higher rate than a bank account, but it has several differences that you may find attractive. First, it has no fixed term: that is, you may withdraw part or all of your money at any time—simply by writing a check against the balance. Second, although its rate of interest payment is not fixed but fluctuates constantly in response to market conditions, it is generally higher, at any given time, than the rate paid by the typical bank CD. This interest can be payable to you by monthly check or it can be automatically reinvested. Lastly, you can make additional deposits or withdrawals at any time, although some funds set deposit minimums from $50 to $250 or more and don't permit withdrawals of less than $250 or $500.

The one disadvantage of money market funds is that, unlike bank CD's they are not insured. But this seems to be a negligible difference because no money market fund depositors have lost their investments during the past ten years or more. In general, if you are reluctant to get involved in stocks and bonds, a money market fund may be your best option. Unlike a CD, it provides some protection against fluctuations in interest rates, although it can't protect your principal against inflation because you get back the same number of dollars that you put in. Even if you decide subsequently to make other investments, you may want to maintain a money market account as a depository for dividends, as a high-interest checking account, and as a parking place for funds between investments.

Mutual Funds

Buying stocks or bonds, as we shall see shortly, can be both hazardous and expensive if your investment is modest. To begin with, you need to pin your faith on only one or two companies and hope that their management and the conditions of the economy will combine to keep them profitable. Second, brokerage commissions or small transactions—100 shares of stock, for example, or a $5,000 bond—can erode your eventual gain or increase your loss.

To help the small investor avoid these disadvantages, a number of investment firms have established mutual funds, which pool the small investments of thousands of customers, buy and sell large blocks of various securities with the funds, and distribute dividends and capital gains to their shareholders after deducting management and advisory fees. Today there are literally thousands of mutual funds, many of them specializing in specific industries, sectors of the economy, or foreign countries.

Buying shares in a mutual fund offers you some immediate advantages. First, instead of buying the stock of a single company, your investment is diversified among many companies, ranging in number from thirty to more than one hundred, and thus your risk is significantly reduced. Second, instead of being forced to buy a "round lot" of at least 100 shares, as you must do on the stock market if you are to keep your commission reasonable, you can make small contributions at any time. Some mutual funds have no minimum for additional investments, and some have minimums of only $50 to $500. And most of them offer automatic reinvestment of all dividends and capital gains.

But there are a couple of disadvantages. For one thing, just as the profitability of a corporation depends on the decisions of its directors and officers, so the success of a mutual fund depends on the decisions of its managers, and these managers have no better claim to infallibility than their corporate counterparts. Although some mutual funds have been conspicuously successful, others have shown disastrous results. And, as we've noted with respect to stock brokers, past performance, no matter how reassuring, is not a thoroughly reliable indicator of future performance.

A second disadvantage has to do with lack of control over the prices at which you buy and sell shares. If you are interested in buying a stock currently selling at 40, you are not obligated to buy it at 40. You can, if you prefer, enter a "good till cancelled" buy order at, say, 37, and your broker will buy the stock for you only if and when it drops to 37. Similarly, you can enter a "good till cancelled" sell order at a higher price than the one currently quoted. But you can't do this with shares of a mutual fund. Although some funds permit you to buy shares by telephone (at the day's closing price), most of them require you to mail off your check in advance. The number of shares your check buys depends on the closing price of the shares on the day your check is received, perhaps three or four days later.

The same problem affects selling. In most cases, you cannot sell shares at a price that you specify. Some funds permit you to sell shares by means of a telephone call—but these shares will be sold at their value at the next market closing after your call. Other funds require a signature-guaranteed letter of instruction for withdrawals—but the selling price is determined at the market closing after your letter has been received. In such a case, the share price may have dropped significantly during the three or four days your letter is in transit. Many mutual fund companies permit you to transfer by telephone money from their mutual stock fund into a money-market fund that they operate, but in general your control over both buy and sell prices is substantially less than it is in stock market transactions.

These disadvantages, however, may be relatively unimportant in connection with a long-term nest egg. If your contributions are spaced out over a period of years, and if dividends are reinvested over the life of the account, the fluctuations in share prices are likely to average out and the assets may grow nicely.

Bonds

Whether it is issued by a government or by a corporation, a bond is essentially a promissory note which, in return for your investment, promises to pay you a specified rate of interest for a specified period of time and then return your initial investment.

Provided that the "borrower" is in good financial health, the likelihood that you will get your initial investment back eventually is fairly good, and this is why bonds seem an obviously safe investment. But there are a couple of hazards that are not so obvious.

To begin with, seemingly healthy corporations—including state and local governments—*have* run into problems that led to default on their bonds. Second, the market today is full of "junk" bonds—bonds that were issued by various investment groups to generate cash for corporate takeovers and are very risky indeed, as indicated by their inordinately high interest rates.

But no matter how vigorous the financial health of the issuer, if the bond is of the long-term variety—and many of them run to twenty or thirty years—you can be certain that inflation will have cut the buying power of your original investment by the time it comes back to you (or your heirs) at maturity. In addition, although you can always sell a bond before maturity, the price you'll get for it depends on general interest rates at the time you sell. If the rates have gone up since you bought the bond, its yield has become less attractive, and you won't get back your full purchase price.

But if interest rates should go down, won't the price of your bond go up? Possibly, but not necessarily, because many bonds are "callable"—that is, their issuer has the right to redeem them at a specified price at specified times. And if interest rates drop far enough to make them an unnecessarily expensive form of borrowing, you can be quite certain that your bond will be called. Not all bonds are callable, but before buying you ought to make sure that the small print doesn't put you into this heads-you-lose, tails-we-win, situation.

Some kinds of bonds have special tax considerations that are relevant for nest eggs. U.S. Treasury EE series bonds yield a satisfactory rate of interest which fluctuates with the prime rate but has a guaranteed minimum. Interest is not paid until the bond matures (in five years) and hence no income tax is due until then. Zero-coupon bonds pay no interest directly; instead, you earn interest by buying the bond at a price substantially below its face value at maturity. However, since you are required to pay income tax each year on the "interest" you don't receive, "zeroes" may be a good investment for a child's money, since he or she is likely to pay no tax or be in a lower bracket than you (see p. 161).

Certain state and municipal bonds are exempt from federal income tax and from income tax in the state in which they are issued. But since the yields of these bonds are generally lower than those of taxable bonds, they are not a good nest-egg investment for a child's custodial account unless its taxable yield will exceed $1,000 a year. Whether they are worthwhile if you keep the nest egg in your own rather than the child's name depends on your tax bracket and the account's current yield.

You can determine whether a tax-free bond is a good investment by using a simple formula:

Interest rate of the bond ÷ (1 − your tax bracket). Then compare the result with the interest rate on a taxable bond.

Thus, if you are in the 28% bracket and you are offered a tax-free bond that pays 6%, the formula 6 ÷ .72 would require that a taxable bond yield at least 8.33% in order to be comparable.

Stocks

When the nest egg is small, buying stocks can be too expensive to be worthwhile, for two reasons. First, unless you buy in "round" lots of 100, the "odd lot" price you pay per share may be slightly higher. Second, the broker's minimum commission, which is based on 100 shares, will have to be spread over fewer shares, both on buying and on selling. Thus, if a stock is selling for, say, $20 and you buy 20 shares, your cost per share, including the commission, will be about $22 at the very least—and the shares will have to appreciate almost 20% before you can break even, because the commission for selling will come close to $2 per share, and the "odd lot" can be bought or sold only at the market price and not a price that you specify.

You can avoid this problem by buying a round lot of 100 shares for yourself and transferring ten or twenty shares per year to your child's nest egg, because changing the registration of shares costs nothing. But this complicates matters should you decide to sell the shares before the entire lot has been transferred.

Investors tend to buy stocks with two goals in mind: income from dividends, and growth in the value of the shares. Neither goal, of course, is certain to be achieved. Although the current dividend rate can be found in the daily newspaper stock tables, there is no guarantee that this rate will continue; even some major public utilities—traditionally stable enough to be regarded as "widows' and orphans'" stocks—have in recent years lowered or suspended their dividend payments.

Growth in share value is equally uncertain, because it depends not only on the corporation's management but on a complex and unpredictable combination of factors, including the national and world economic situation, interest rates, and technological change.

Although the almost uninterrupted boom in the stock market during the 1980s made many investors rich, stock prices have, in recent years, become decidedly volatile. *In the long run,* however, investment in stocks has been more rewarding than any other kind of investment. Since your child's nest egg is destined for the long run, stocks may constitute an important part of it.

Options, Commodities, Futures, Gold, Etc.

Proponents of the stock market like to create the impression that in buying stock you are investing in "America's industrial productivity" or some such worthy goal. This may be true on the rare occasion when investors buy new shares of stock issued by a fledgling company in need of capital for rapid expansion. But the vast majority of stock trades have nothing to do with the company named on the stock certificate. They are nothing more than bets, with the buyer betting that the share price will go up and the seller betting that it will go down.

Does this kind of betting differ from what goes on in Las Vegas or Atlantic City? In some respects it does. To begin with, it's legal in all states. Moreover, it does not depend entirely on chance; a certain amount of research and study can help you increase your gains and reduce your losses. And, lastly, although you may suffer losses, your wager is unlikely to be wiped out completely.

But certain kinds of stock-market transactions are more dependent on luck than others, because there is no way of basing your investment decision on any kind of reliable information. Because you can't possibly predict, for example, whether the price of wheat or cotton or pork bellies will go up or down within the next several months, an investment in "commodity futures" is as much dependent on luck as a game of blackjack at a casino.

The same is true of options to buy or sell a certain stock at some time in the future—a strategy that holds out the promise of substantial gains in return for a low investment. Again, you have no way of predicting whether the stock will go up or down. If you own the stock itself, you can sell it if it goes up or keep it if it goes down, hoping that it will recover. But if you guess wrong on an option, you simply lose your money. Just as you would not take a substantial part of your child's nest egg to Atlantic City in the hope of tripling it in an afternoon, the same thinking should keep you away from these speculative investments.

DIVERSIFYING FOR SAFETY

The only sure way of picking a winner in a horse race is to bet on every horse. This system won't work at the race track, of course, because your losses will exceed your winnings. But because a reasonably prudent investment, unlike a bet on a horse, is unlikely to be wiped out, the principle of diversification is a good one. Instead of putting all your child's nest egg into one basket, you can spread the risk by putting some of it in cash, some in bonds, and some in stocks.

Within these general categories, you can diversify further. The cash, for example, might be divided between CDs and money market funds, the bonds between industrial and government, the stock between mutuals, blue chips, and more speculative issues. This kind of diversification requires you to do more monitoring of the market and more bookkeeping than putting all your child's money on a "sure thing." But "sure things" are as rare on the investment scene as they are at the race track.

TWO FURTHER ALTERNATIVES

Two further investment options—one old, the other relatively new, and both superficially attractive—need careful scrutiny before you decide to make them components of your child's nest egg.

Life Insurance Policy
for the Child

The first sales pitch likely to come your way—often within a few days of the child's birth—is for an insurance policy on the life of the child. This will take either of two forms: (1) a policy that, in addition to providing the child with life insurance, matures after a specified period of time (usually twenty years) and pays off an accumulated cash amount to the child, or (2) a policy that can be continued indefinitely by the child at the original low monthly premium.

There are several reasons why the first type of policy is sure to be a poor investment. If you assume (in most cases correctly) that the child will survive the twenty-year period and collect the cash accumulation, the earnings on the premiums will turn out to be disappointingly low—because inflation is likely to have eroded the face value, because insurance companies are niggardly in paying returns, and because part of the premiums has gone to pay for the life insurance coverage. The life insurance coverage itself is of negligible value, because after the first year or two of the child's life (during which the coverage is limited to only a small fraction of the policy's face value), the childhood years are the healthiest and safest of his entire lifetime, and the chances of collecting the face value are very small indeed. More important, would a cash payment really console you upon the death of your child? If so, you can get this kind of consolation by considering the money you save by not having to support him until adulthood or beyond!

As for taking advantage of the low initial premium to initiate a "whole life" policy, there are two objections. To begin with, the amount of coverage your child will need when he or she is an adult will depend not only on his personal situation but on the effects of twenty years of inflation, and neither factor is predictable. As a result, what may look to you like a generous endowment for the child may turn out, when the child is in her or his twenties or thirties, to be a trivial amount.

In light of these disadvantages, why do these childhood policies retain their popularity? They are bought primarily by parents who require monthly premium notices and the threat of policy lapse as incentives to save systematically and by grandparents who feel that they are making a generous gift at the cost of rather small monthly premiums. But neither of these buyers evaluates the policy critically as an investment. Those who do are almost certain to reject it.

College Prepayment Plans—Pay Now, Learn Later

A number of colleges and universities, out of concern for their current cash flow problems and their future enrollments, have begun to offer parents of young children the opportunity to make an immediate lump-sum payment or periodic payments in advance for the four years of room-board-and-tuition costs that their child will face some 18 years in the future. One private college, for example, guarantees four years of full tuition 18 years hence in exchange for an immediate cash payment only 24% above its current tuition charge for a single year. (The children of alumni get a $400 discount.)

On the face of it, this arrangement offers several advantages. First, unlike you, the college (because it is a tax-exempt institution) can invest the money tax-free, and tax-free compounding can make a relatively small initial down payment grow rapidly enough to cover those projected costs. Second, the college may have access to financial advice—and to investments—that you, as a small investor, can't afford. In addition, it protects you against increases in college costs, which are currently rising faster than the general rate of inflation. And, lastly, because neither the lump-sum nor the periodic payments are overwhelmingly large, a generous grandparent may find this a very effective way of ensuring the child's college education.

There are, however, some obvious drawbacks. Although the possibility may strike you as unthinkable, it's conceivable that your child will turn out not to be "college material" (the colleges don't guarantee admission) or may decide against college even if he or she is. On the other hand, she or he may win a National Merit Scholarship and be courted with further scholarships by some of the most selective schools in the country. There is also the danger that the college making the prepayment offer doesn't (or won't) have the kind of curriculum that the child will want almost two decades from now. And there is even the possibility that the college may have closed its doors by the time your child is ready to apply. Worse yet, some colleges offer no refunds, and some will refund your principal only. In any event, as we note in Chapter 6, the child should participate in the choice of a college, and the degree of participation of which an infant is capable is clearly limited.

Of course, some of these objections are less applicable to offers like the one made by the state of Michigan, which operates a dozen or more institutions whose admissions standards vary as widely as their curriculums, which permits use of the funds in some of the state's private colleges, and which provides for a partial refund if the child decides against college. However, the MET (Michigan Education Trust) program is currently closed to new contracts, and some have questioned its future solvency. Before involving yourself in any plan of this kind, you ought therefore to find out about the conditions governing a refund, and then compare the deal with what you could earn by putting the same money aside, even though you may be taxed on the yield.

Another prepayment plan is offered by banks and other financial institutions. For a set schedule of payments beginning during the child's very early years, these institutions guarantee four years of college tuition at a public college or university when the child is ready for it, no matter how high the cost has risen.

Such plans look attractive because their sponsors inevitably exaggerate the cost of higher education, extrapolating over the next two decades the rather sharp increases experienced during the past several years. Overlooked in this calculation is the fact that society as a whole has a very strong interest in developing an educated citizenry and therefore will find ways to keep a college education within reach of the children of parents with moderate or low incomes.

WILLS, GUARDIANSHIPS, AND TAX STRATEGIES

The fairly tranquil last trimester of pregnancy and the early weeks of infancy, when your baby spends 16 to 18 hours a day sleeping peacefully, offer a good opportunity to take care of a number of matters which you may be too busy to deal with later on. But because none of them may have struck you as urgent at that time, you may well have put them off to another day. In that case, it's a good idea to attend to them now, because further procrastination can create problems. At best, you may find yourself forced to take care of them in a thoughtless hurry; at worst, you may be too late to do anything at all.

MAKING A WILL

If you haven't yet bothered to make a will, you have a great deal of company. Three out of four Americans die without one. And your own procrastination may stem from the same reasons: You don't have enough assets to make it worth the trouble. You'll get around to it later. You don't like to think about death.

None of these arguments is very sound. To begin with, you probably have more assets than you realize: the equity of your home, your car, your personal belongings, money owed to you, even the possibility that you hold a winning lottery ticket or that your death in an accident will result in a "wrongful death" claim worth a million dollars. The I'm-not-going-to-die-very-soon argument is equally shaky. Even though the death rate for your age group is reassuringly low, these actuarial statistics won't help you if a drunk driver crashes into your car head-on or your doctor diagnoses that skin wart as malignant, or a construction crane collapses as you walk past it on your way to lunch. Nobody likes to think about death, but it is nevertheless a fact of life.

If you die without a will, all assets owned by you alone—that is, those not held in joint tenancy with your spouse (see p. 190)—will pass not necessarily to the people you prefer but to those specified as your "heirs at law" by the laws of your state. In most states, this means that if you die, up to half of your solely owned assets will go to your spouse and the other half to your children (with your spouse as their guardian if they are minors)—an arrangement that may be precisely what you had in mind. But if you are a single parent, or if you are cohabiting with someone without the formality of legal marriage, or if you want all your solely owned assets to go to your spouse, the disposal of your assets becomes unbelievably complicated—and almost certainly *not* what you would prefer. And, no matter what your marital status, in the absence of a will, you can leave nothing to a more distant relative, a friend, or a charity.

But a will does more than direct the distribution of your assets. Its second function—and one that may be far more important for parents—is to designate a guardian for your minor children. And so, no matter how few your assets or how small your net worth, making a will is essential to ensure that custody of your orphaned minor children passes to the person you prefer.

Naming a Guardian

If you or your spouse should die suddenly, the survivor will, of course, retain responsibility for bringing up your child and, although spouse and child will miss the deceased spouse's presence and income, at least part of their loss can be alleviated by adequate life insurance coverage. But what if you are a single parent? Or what if both you and your spouse die simultaneously? Although it may strike you as extremely improbable, husbands and wives do die together in automobile accidents, plane crashes, and fires. And until you reach the age of forty, you are more likely to die in an accident than from any other cause.

In such circumstances, who will be responsible for rearing your minor child to adulthood? From birth to the age of majority, your child is, in the eyes of the law, an "infant" or a "minor" and is not allowed to engage in many essential activities of life without the authorization of a parent or, in the absence of a parent, a formally designated guardian. For example, a minor cannot get medical or dental treatment, or register for school, or go on field trips, or play on an athletic team without parental consent. Later on, he will not be permitted to dispose of certain kinds of property or to marry or to join the armed forces without parental (or a guardian's) approval. The guardian must, of course, be an adult—and this is why novels and television programs in which the orphaned fifteen-year-old daughter heroically brings up her younger siblings are sheer fiction.

If you and your spouse should die without having designated a guardian in a will, the probate court will appoint one. But because the court almost invariably assumes that "blood runs thicker than water," it will usually appoint a brother or sister of one of the parents. This arrangement may strike you as perfectly satisfactory but, on the other hand, it may not. Actually, a guardian has two functions, and the person selected by the court may not be ideally suited to carry out one or both of them.

The most important function of a guardian is to act *in loco parentis*—that is, to bring up your minor child in the same way that you would—in terms of the style of discipline used, the education and recreational opportunities provided, and the values and behavior taught. It's quite possible that a relative would be the person you would choose to carry on where you left off, but it's also conceivable that your own values, aspirations, standard of living, and style of child-rearing are very different from those of a brother or sister and that a close friend would be much more congenial. If so, your will should designate the friend and not leave the decision to the court.

The second function of a guardian is economic—that is, to bring up the child at a standard of living that you are now able to provide or that you hope to provide in the future. And unless you have substantial assets or life insurance enough to cover the costs of this, you may be imposing on the guardian an almost intolerable financial burden.

In the absence of sufficient insurance coverage, these economic obligations of guardianship can pose a dilemma: should you appoint as guardian your warm, loving sister, who has a fine relationship with your child but is hard-pressed financially, or should you select your well-to-do brother-in-law, whom your child doesn't like very much and who is a tougher disciplinarian than you? Or is there a friend of yours who is not only warm and loving but also reasonably well-to-do?

In such circumstances your choice of a guardian requires not only careful thought but a large measure of tact and diplomacy in your approach to the person you'd like to designate. Some of the people you consider may think of a guardianship as a largely honorific position—rather like that of a godmother or godfather. And so, feeling flattered, they may accept your invitation without recognizing the heavy economic responsibilities it entails. Others may understand the responsibilities but feel uncomfortable about turning you down. Still others may be hurt because you have *not* nominated them.

Often the problem can be solved by a reciprocal arrangement with friends or relatives who are also parents: we'll serve as guardians for your kids if you'll do the same for ours. Of course, it's important to bear in mind with respect to guardianships that many are called but few are chosen. The likelihood that the guardian you designate will ever have to assume his role is very, very remote.

But even if you leave ample life insurance or other assets, some problems may remain. Your warm and loving sister may be in poor shape financially because she and her husband manage money badly. Should you, then, entrust her with the assets intended for your child? You don't doubt that she would respect the legal requirement that she use your money for—and only for—the benefit of your child, but will she invest it productively or spend it unwisely? And would your hard-nosed but financially astute brother-in-law manage the money more efficiently?

In such a situation, there are two solutions. You can designate in your will, in addition to a guardian of the child's person, a conservator of the child's inheritance. Or you can establish a trust to receive and manage your child's inheritance.

Conservators

Unlike a guardian of the child's person, a conservator is responsible only for taking care of all assets that you and others leave to your child and for making periodic payments to the guardian, from principal or earnings, to meet the costs of rearing your child. In theory this arrangement gives you the best of both worlds. Your warm, loving sister will rear your child according to your values. And your cold-fish brother-in-law can use his financial know-how to get the maximum yield from your child's assets and to preserve—and perhaps even increase—their value. If you don't have this kind of brother-in-law, your will can designate a bank, a trust company, or a responsible friend as conservator.

But in practice such an arrangement has limitations. To begin with, the conservator is required to function under the close supervision of the probate court and must get the court's permission for every major transaction or investment. And the courts, understandably more concerned with preserving the assets than with increasing their value, tend to be quite conservative about approving investments. The court may, for example, insist that all assets be deposited in federally insured institutions, even though the conservator could invest them elsewhere much more productively with very little sacrifice of safety. For this reason, people who are astute in managing money tend to become unbearably frustrated by the restrictions they face as conservators.

Worse yet, a conservatorship comes to an end automatically when your child reaches majority (age 18 in most states), at which time all the assets are turned over to the child. If at that time your child is too immature to use the money wisely—if she or he decides to buy a Corvette instead of a college education, or to use the money as working capital in the illicit-drug business—there is nothing that the conservator or anyone else can do about it.

Given these limitations, parents who expect to leave their children only moderate assets usually designate the guardian as the conservator as well—provided that he is trustworthy enough not to use the assets for his own benefit and orderly enough not to leave dividend checks lying around uncashed for months. True, a guardianship, like a conservatorship, terminates when the minor attains the age of majority, but if the assets are not substantial, the danger of their being dissipated is not serious. On the other hand, parents who are likely to bequeath substantial assets and are concerned with protecting their child against his own immaturity should consider establishing a trust, which is not only more flexible and more versatile than a conservatorship, but provides the only means by which distribution of funds to the children can be postponed beyond the age of majority.

The Testamentary Trust

One device that can avert the possibility that your child will squander his inheritance is the testamentary trust—a trust that your lawyer can incorporate into your will. Under such an arrangement, all assets (or whatever part of them you specify) pass, at your death, into the trust, which is managed by a trustee—a relative, a friend, a bank or trust company, or anyone else you designate—for the benefit of your survivors.

In this will-created trust, you can specify virtually any conditions or restrictions you like about the child's use of the money. You can, for example, withhold all the money until the child reaches a specified age, you can stipulate that the earnings but not the principal will be paid out to the child for a certain number of years, you can require that payments out of principal may be made only for specified purposes (college expenses, for example) or that the child is to receive annually from the trust fund an amount not exceeding what he is earning through his own efforts. This kind of trust is immortal. It can continue just as long as you specify or until its assets are exhausted.

As we shall see in Chapter 11, trusts are available in several forms and serve many useful purposes in addition to what we've described here. But at this stage of your life, the testamentary trust is likely to be the simplest and most economical estate-planning instrument that serves your immediate needs.

Drawing Up a Will

For most people, a do-it-yourself will is not a good idea because state laws governing wills are complex, and a homemade version may be declared invalid on the basis of a petty technicality. A few states (California, Maine, Michigan, and Wisconsin) make available to their residents standard will forms that conform to their laws, but, in general, the typical attorney's fee for a simple will—usually $100 to $300—is well worth paying for the assurance that your will is comprehensive, completely valid, and properly executed.

Because an attorney's fee is based on the time he spends with you, you can save money by preparing yourself for the visit with a complete list of your assets, a list of your intended beneficiaries, your designation of the executor, guardian, and conservator or trustee, and—perhaps most important—a list of "what if?" questions about the naming of contingent beneficiaries and contingent guardians.

Bear in mind that your will is almost certain to need revision as your family situation changes with the passage of time—when, for example, your eldest child reaches majority—and as you acquire more (and more complex) assets. If, at the moment, your assets are few and simple, your will can be correspondingly short and simple, and a more complex disposition of your assets can be postponed until you have more of them. But this should not induce you to postpone making and signing a will. Its guardianship function is crucial right now, although it may vanish by the time the growth of your assets requires you to make a new one.

MANAGING YOUR CHILD'S INCOME

As long as your child is an "infant," the law exempts him from many responsibilities and obligations. Not so the IRS. It requires him (or you on his behalf) to file an income tax return for any year (including the year of his birth) in which he receives any of the following income:

- investment income (from interest, dividends, capital gains, etc.) of more than $600
- earned income (from wages and self employment, e.g., newspaper route, baby-sitting, lawn-mowing, etc.) of more than $3,700 (in 1993)

These figures may strike you as irrelevant if you think about the earning power of your six-month-old daughter, but if you or her grandparents give her gifts or securities amounting to more than $10,000, their yield can easily approach or exceed her $600 standard deduction. If the prospect of your child's having to file a return seems imminent, your first step is to obtain a Social Security number for her, even though by law she is not required to have one until age one.

Obtaining a Social Security Number for Children

To obtain a Social Security number for your child, you must file with your local Social Security office IRS Form No. SS-5 along with an original or certified copy of the child's birth certificate and one additional document establishing the parents' identity: a hospital bill, vaccination certificate, newspaper birth announcement, adoption record, etc. These documents will be returned to you.

If your child was born outside the United States and is not a citizen, you must submit an original birth certificate or passport plus documents issued by the U.S. Immigration and Naturalization Service establishing that he or she has been legally admitted.

If you need to file an income tax return for the child before you receive the Social Security number, simply write "Applied for" in the appropriate space.

Custodial Account for Minors

At a child's birth, and on subsequent birthdays and other significant occasions, it's not unusual for grandparents and other relatives to make gifts to the child in the form of cash—sometimes in substantial amounts. As we noted in Chapter 2, you can accumulate these gifts in a nest egg registered in your own name and informally earmarked for the child's future use, but doing this makes you liable for income tax on the yield of these gifts. You can shift this tax liability to your child (whose tax bracket is almost certain to be lower than yours) by establishing what is known as a custodial account.

The Custodial Account for Minors has been so popular for so many years that in your own childhood you may have played the role of "minor" with a parent or grandparent as the "custodian." The reason for its popularity is not hard to see: when custodial accounts were first authorized, the income tax on their yield was payable entirely by the minor, who, since his other income amounted to little or nothing, either paid a minimum tax or no tax at all. Thus, instead of building a nest egg for their child and paying income tax on its yield, the parents who established a custodial account paid no tax on it at all. And the minor paid no tax unless the account balance was so large that its yield exceeded the minor's tax exemption. Under this arrangement, most minors paid no tax at all.

But the Tax Reform Act of 1986 stripped the custodial account of much of its tax advantage. Today, until the child reaches the age of 14, he is liable for tax on the first $1,200 of yield at his tax rate but the balance of the yield is taxable at the top tax rate paid by his parents. Once the minor turns 14, he is still liable for tax on the entire yield, but at his own tax rate, which, presumably, is lower than that of his parents.

Some parents and grandparents have deplored this tightening of the tax benefit, but it would appear that those deploring it most bitterly are the very rich, because the custodial account still provides considerable tax advantage for parents of moderate means. The fact remains that you would have to deposit about $20,000 into a custodial account for an infant who receives no other income before the yield would exceed her $1,200 exemption and be subject to the new "kiddie" tax. On the other hand, if you were to keep the same $20,000 in your own nest egg, you would pay at least $280 in taxes for each $1,000 in yield. Even if, after age 14, the child's income makes the yield from the account subject to tax, it is likely to be taxed at her 15-percent bracket rather than your higher bracket—a saving of at least $130 per $1,000 of yield. Of course, if you can afford to, you can exceed the hypothetical $20,000 deposit in the custodial account by any amount you like without jeopardizing the tax savings if you add the increment in the form of tax-exempt municipal bonds or investments for which the income is deferred to a date beyond the child's fourteenth birthday.

A custodial account can be viewed as an income-yielding piggy-bank into which you can deposit assets that you intend to accumulate for the benefit of the child. If you establish it in a bank, credit union, or savings-and-loan association, setting it up costs nothing, there is usually no minimum for initial or subsequent deposits, nor is there any obligation to make regular deposits periodically. A custodial account with a stockbroker or a mutual fund costs nothing to set up, and the securities may be issued in the custodian's name or held by the broker in an account established by the custodian.

There is no limit to the number of custodial accounts either you, your spouse, the child's grandparents, or any other person can establish (for the same child or for several). One of the custodial accounts, for example, might be a passbook savings account into which you deposit periodic small contributions plus, perhaps, the occasional windfall. As the balance grows, you can transfer some or all of the funds into a higher-yielding certificate of deposit or a brokerage or mutual fund account registered in the form of a custodial account.

Custodial accounts are available everywhere because every state has adopted either the Uniform Gifts to Minors Act or the Uniform Transfers to Minors Act, which authorize the use of custodial accounts for minors. Thus, to open a custodial account for your child, all you need do is fill out the bank's signature card, the treasury bond registration, or the brokerage or mutual fund account application as "John Jones, custodian for John Jones Jr. under the Uniform Gifts to Minors Act [your state]." On stock certificates, brokers' statements, and mutual fund documents, this may appear in more cryptic abbreviation as "John Jones CUST John Jones, Jr., UGMA [Mich]." All custodial accounts carry, as the "taxpayer's identification number," your child's social security number (see p. 55).

The major advantage of the custodial account is, as we've seen, the shifting of tax liability on its yield from the custodian to the minor. What, then, are the disadvantages? They stem from the rules and restrictions built into the Uniform Gift to Minors Act. To begin with, funds in the account may be used only for the benefit of the minor, not the custodian. This means that you may not borrow from the account to meet personal emergencies or use the money for any purpose of your own. Furthermore, you may not use the principal or the income to pay expenses of the minor that are part of a parent's "ordinary" responsibilities.

Although the Act does not distinguish specifically between ordinary and extraordinary expenses, it is generally interpreted to mean that you may not use the funds to pay for the child's food, clothing, shelter, medical care, or any other expense that parents are expected to meet, but that you may legitimately draw from the custodial account to pay for music lessons, summer camp, orthodontia, trips to Europe, college costs, and other activities to which every child is not normally entitled. This, then, is the primary disadvantage of the custodial account: although you may shift funds from one custodial account to another, what you deposit in it stays there for keeps and remains beyond your reach as far as your personal use is concerned.

The second disadvantage may be already familiar to you from our discussion of guardianships and conservatorships. On the day the minor reaches the age of majority—eighteen in all but a few states—the custodian is obligated to turn the assets over to him or her on demand. And if, at that time, the minor decides to use them to finance a year in Nepal instead of four years at Yale, he is legally entitled to do so—as some dismayed parents and other donors have discovered.

There are only two ways to prevent this takeover of the assets: you can keep the existence of the account a secret until the child shows signs of maturity and responsibility or, instead of a custodial account, you can establish a trust for minors.

Trusts for Minors

A trust for minors, known also as a Section 503(c) trust (in reference to the section of the Internal Revenue Code that authorizes it), differs from a custodial account in four respects, any of which may be attractive to you: (1) it withholds the assets from the minor until age 21 instead of 18; (2) you, as the person funding the trust (or the trustee if you appoint one and empower him or her to do so), may incorporate into the trust document the same sorts of conditions that you can stipulate in a testamentary trust: how much money should be paid out to the minor, at what intervals, for what purposes, and so forth; (3) once he attains majority the former minor may, if he or she feels that the trust is being managed productively, continue it indefinitely while drawing some income from it; (4) it can include several minors rather than only one; and (5) it can own real estate as well as any other assets.

In general, a trust for minors is worthwhile only if the assets you intend for your child's future use are (or will be) so substantial that management by a professional trustee seems a good idea. The tax advantages are likely to be less attractive than those of a custodial account: the minor pays taxes on any income she draws from the trust; the trust itself pays taxes on the balance. Although you'll need the help of a lawyer to set up the trust, and although you may want to designate a bank or trust company as trustee and pay an annual fee for its services, there is no reason why you can't serve as your own trustee if you have the time and skill necessary to manage the trust assets.

On the other hand, the lifetime of a trust for minors is limited, since it terminates when the minor reaches the age of 21. You can accomplish most of the purposes of a trust for minors by incorporating its provisions in a living, or *inter vivos,* trust, which is far more useful, flexible, and long-lived. Because it is more often used in connection with estate planning than with nest-egg building, we discuss this very useful instrument in Chapter 11.

Yet Another Tax

But income-tax liability for the nest egg is not your only concern. Whether you have structured it in the form of a custodial account or a trust for minors, the IRS concludes that you have, in effect, made a gift to a minor and hence you may be liable for the tax which the federal government imposes on gifts of a certain size. Gifts of less than $10,000 per year ($20,000 if made with the consent of your spouse) are tax exempt, but gifts of $10,000/$20,000 or more must be reported to the IRS by filing a federal gift tax return, and the tax on them will be charged against your lifetime exemption (see p. 193). But since very few parents of young children are either willing or able to make gifts of this size, we postpone further discussion to Chapter 11.

Keeping Your Child's Records

One chore that is all too easily postponed is the setting up of a file or storage space for your child's important records. A cardboard file box that can accommodate half a dozen manila file folders will suffice, with the folders labeled more or less as follows:

Birth/baptismal records

Medical, dental, and optical records

Social Security records

Tax returns

Investments

School records

Keepsakes: letters, recital programs, awards, etc.

Once established and used conscientiously, such an arrangement can eliminate both the risk of loss and a frantic search each time you urgently need to retrieve something.

Part II

OUT-OF-POCKET
EXPENSES

In the normal course of events, you can expect to support your child from birth until he or she is at least part of the way through college—and perhaps even longer. But although this long-term responsibility is continuous, its actual costs will change over time, and so will your ability to meet them. During the first twelve years of your child's life, your out-of-pocket expenses will be relatively low and your income is likely to increase, especially if one spouse begins or resumes working at some time after the child's birth. This early stage, then, is a good time for building the nest egg that you will need for the considerably greater expenses that you will inevitably encounter when the child reaches his teens.

As your child grows, so do the costs of maintaining him or her. As his appetite and his need for privacy increase, your outlays for food and shelter increase correspondingly. A serious interest in a performing art may make lessons, instruments, and other equipment loom larger on your budget. And, although once he played happily on the kitchen floor with pots and pans, his "toys" may come to include a ten-speed bicycle or a computer—or both. And, inevitably, there is the cost of college—preceded, perhaps, by a parent-subsidized trip to Europe.

But this state of affairs is not so grim as it may appear. As the years pass, you can reasonably assume that your earned income will increase to some extent through cost-of-living increases, merit raises—and perhaps both. So too will what the IRS calls your "unearned" income—that is, the yield from investments and other assets. And by the time your child has graduated from high school, many of your other major purchases—vehicles, home furnishings and appliances, perhaps a boat or a summer cottage—will probably have been paid for and your home mortgage may be nearing its end. Hence, although college costs may still seem intimidating, you may well have more disposable income than you anticipate.

You are more likely to achieve this relatively worry-free state if you adopt the kind of disciplined program of nest-egg building that we have described in Chapter 2. But you are more likely to take kindly to the necessary self-discipline if you were to have a "road map" indicating the ordinary and extraordinary out-of-pocket expenditures that lie ahead as your child moves from the obstetric ward to the college campus. This map, with the highway hazards clearly marked, is contained in Chapters 4 and 5.

CHAPTER 4

THE EARLY YEARS

If all goes normally, the years between infancy and the child's twelfth birthday need not involve huge outlays. The month or two following the child's birth may be expensive if the mother requires paid help with household activities, but this is a short-term matter. For the longer term, you can expect a higher level of medical costs for such routine matters as shots and check-ups, and perhaps an initial outlay for orthodontia, but some of these costs can be met by good health-insurance coverage.

Day-care costs, as we shall see, can be substantial, but presumably there will be two incomes to meet them. Toys and other playthings will be an ongoing expense but not a major one, since you won't have to reckon with $500 clarinets or $400 cameras until your child is into her teens. Private lessons in music, dance, or art can burden your budget, but only if your local school system doesn't provide such instruction at little or no cost. Private schooling, too, can be very expensive, but it is actually necessary far less frequently than parents seem to think.

Because lifestyles and incomes vary so widely, it would be presumptuous of us to offer dollars-and-cents advice on how much to spend and what to spend it on. Instead, we shall deal with items and issues that confront almost all parents, no matter what their income level or their style of child-rearing.

INFANCY ACCESSORIES

Because having a baby—especially the first one—is a joyous occasion, many parents celebrate it with extravagant expenditures on various kinds of nursery equipment: cribs, playpens, highchairs, swings, prams, and strollers. And manufacturers and retailers exploit the new parents' exuberant extravagance with a tempting array of unnecessarily expensive models. As a consequence, you may, unless you are careful, find yourself investing hundreds of dollars in "capital goods" which will have a useful life of only a year or two.

Doting grandparents often make the same mistake. Especially if your baby has provided their first experience in the role, they are likely to express their pleasure with gifts of equipment that they feel you could not afford. If you know that this is likely, you may be able to persuade them, without hurting their feelings, that a Series EE Treasury bond or an initial deposit in a custodial account (see p. 55) would be a more welcome gift for the baby than a $200 baby carriage or playpen.

You can avoid overspending if you recognize that an infant has no esthetic sense and will sleep just as soundly and comfortably in a ten-dollar secondhand crib as in a brand new hundred-dollar model—and that a baby carriage isn't worth a premium price for its value as a status symbol. Making do with second- or third-hand equipment, as long as it's clean, safe, and sturdy, can save you a good deal of money and cost you almost nothing in satisfaction.

The most productive source of used equipment may be friends, relatives, or neighbors who are two or three years ahead of you in the child-rearing process. Lacking these, you might scan the classified ads in the local newspaper. Another good source may be the P.T.A. thrift shop in your own or a neighboring community. Once you've had a good thrift shop experience with baby equipment, you may be motivated to return later for bargains in outgrown high-quality clothing, toys, skates, skis, and other items that have too short a useful life to be worth buying brand new.

DAY CARE

If your family is typical, the annual cost of child care during your working years will run between $5,000 and $8,500 (for a child under three years of age)—the most expensive item on your budget after housing and taxes. But whether or not you worry about its cost, the prospect of entrusting the care of your child to someone else may make you feel a bit guilty. Women whose earnings are used to buy "extras" rather than necessities—or to pay for the costs of child care—often feel that their decision to work is a selfish one, that they are somehow abdicating the responsibilities of parenthood by gratifying their own interests instead of staying home to mother their child, and that the child is likely to develop serious problems later in life as a result of being brought up by strangers.

But this guilt may be altogether groundless. A good day-care center can offer the child far more in the way of social skills, recreational activities, and preparation for later schooling than parents can provide at home. And, if the findings of a number of studies are valid, children who enter kindergarten after a year or two of high-quality day-care experience turn out to be far more "successful"—socially, emotionally, and intellectually—than those who come directly from home.

But *good* day care is not easy to find. Although the increase in single-parent households and the vast influx of women into the work force in recent years has created an enormous demand, the supply shows no signs of catching up with it—and for understandable reasons.

To begin with, high-quality child care is inevitably expensive. It requires safe, centrally located facilities that comply with the state's licensing requirements, liability insurance, good playground and other recreational equipment, space and equipment for meals and naps, and, perhaps most important, a very low child:teacher ratio—as low as four children per teacher when the children are very young.

In addition, the care-givers should have training (preferably at the college level) in child development and early childhood education. But because hours are long, the pay low, and the work often hard, emotionally and physically, people with the appropriate training are generally attracted to kindergarten or elementary-school teaching rather than day-care work. Improving the salaries and easing the working conditions might attract or retain good care-givers, but it would raise the costs far beyond what most parents could afford.

A few large corporations, recognizing that the availability of good day-care does much to increase the stability and productivity of their employees, offer some kind of day-care subsidy as part of their fringe benefit packages. Some maintain on-site day-care facilities; others provide financial assistance; still others offer a counseling and referral service. In addition, some churches and social agencies have established day-care facilities in church basements and community centers on a nonprofit basis, with a sliding scale of fees based on parent income and the balance of their budgets paid by contributions from United Way or the local, state, or federal government.

Some public school systems have extended day-care programs which, for a moderate fee, take care of children before and after school while the parents work. There are also, in larger communities, some private, for-profit day-care centers but, because good day care is inevitably expensive, these are likely to charge very high fees or hire less qualified staff with a very high turnover rate.

Checking Out a Day-Care Center

Your chances of finding a satisfactory day-care center depend, then, not only on what you can afford to pay but also on what is available in your community and, because of the general scarcity, a single day-care center in your community may represent "the only game in town." But even if this is the case you need to examine the center critically instead of signing on gratefully.

Although you may be able to get some information from friends and neighbors, the best source is your own impressions—gained by visiting during a routine day and spending at least an hour observing what goes on. As we shall see shortly, there are a number of alternatives to the conventional day-care center and, although each has its limitations, one of them may be more satisfactory than a day-care center that fails to meet some criteria that are important to you.

State Licensure Because most states require day-care centers to be licensed, you can get a great deal of information rather quickly by writing to the state commission for a copy of its licensure requirements. These usually cover such matters as fire safety, emergency medical care, insurance coverage, playground equipment, food service, staff qualifications, transportation equipment, sanitary facilities—and, in some states, even the construction and thickness of the children's napping mattresses.

Although strict licensing requirements have been criticized on the grounds that the cost of compliance prevents elderly widows and low-budget social agencies from starting up a day-care facility, and although some states with strict requirements don't enforce them by frequent and unscheduled inspections, the fact is that sensible licensing standards offer you and your child substantial protection. Even if inspections are lax, reputable centers are likely to comply with the law. And if you find something to complain about after your child is enrolled, your complaint will get much prompter action if it stems from the center's violation of a license requirement.

Child-rearing Style Because your child may spend more hours each day with day-care staff than with you and your spouse, the *in loco parentis* role of the staff can become rather powerful—and your child's behavior may be influenced as much by them as by you. For this reason it is important to find out—not only by asking questions but by direct observation during a visit—what goes on between staff and children and between the children themselves.

Although only a few of them administer corporal punishment (with parental authorization), day-care centers do differ in their style of child-rearing. Some are very strict and expect prompt obedience as well as neatness and "proper" behavior; others are extremely permissive about the normal messiness of young children and their natural tendencies to settle disputes through the use of physical force, name-calling, and "dirty" words. Whatever your own philosophy, it's important to make sure that the center's style won't conflict with yours. Otherwise the child is likely to become confused by differences between your standards and what he or she learns during the day.

Staff Quality Although state licensing requirements can specify the "on paper" minimum qualifications of the day-care staff, they cannot specify criteria for staff personality or motivation. But an interview with the director should help you decide whether or not he or she is a dedicated, enthusiastic, and well-trained professional who genuinely likes what she is doing and is able to recruit a loyal and capable staff. And your observation of the ongoing activities can tell you much about the warmth, patience, and skill of the staff. The rate of staff turnover is also significant. Because many of the staff members are professionals in the early stages of their career, some annual turnover is inevitable, but a high rate at midyear indicates administrative problems and possibly inconsistent care that can seriously disrupt children's lives.

Work or Play? Some day-care centers—notably those in university towns or in neighborhoods populated by highly educated parents—stress "academic" skills, such as reading readiness and experience with numbers, even for two-year-olds, the assumption being that this kind of program will give children a head start once they enter school. Others favor the development of social and manual skills and deliberately avoid anything that smacks of "school." And still others are essentially baby-sitting operations with no discernible program or philosophy. The "academic" programs have been criticized for putting premature pressure on the child, but the purely custodial programs have been criticized even more severely for functioning simply as holding tanks.

Activity Range A good daily program not only alternates between indoor and outdoor activities and provides ample equipment for both but also schedules field trips and other activities away from the center. Urban centers can make use of the many resources a city provides—not only zoos and museums but also supermarkets and shopping centers—to give the children direct experience with the routines of daily living. Many rural centers use vans or buses to take the children to see dairy farming, maple-sugar production, sheepshearing, beekeeping, and other local activities.

Hours of Operation If your child is of school age, the center's daily, monthly, and holiday schedule can be important, because many minor holidays observed by the public schools may not be observed by employers. In addition, you need to inquire about what happens to the child if you are delayed at work for an hour or two beyond the usual pick-up time.

Parental Participation At some day-care centers parents participate actively—sometimes formulating policy as members of the board of directors, sometimes by contributing physical work in painting or remodeling the center, sometimes by group discussions of the program, sometimes by public fund-raising. Other centers discourage participation and are run entirely by the professional staff. Your personal preference is important. Will you feel shut out at a nonparticipation center? Or will you begrudge the time you may be expected to contribute at a center that makes parental participation almost obligatory? In either case, is there enough participation to maintain good communication with the staff?

The Costs of Day Care

If you and your spouse both work—or if you are a single custodial parent—the IRS allows you a tax credit for a percentage of your child-care costs for dependent children under age 13. If your adjusted gross income is $10,000 or less, you'll be allowed to deduct 30% of your costs—to a maximum of $2,400 for one child and $4,800 for two or more. If your adjusted gross income is more than $10,000, the 30% credit is reduced by 1% for each additional $2,000 of income but does not drop below 20% regardless of your income. Qualifying expenses include sums paid for household services and for the care of a qualifying child in the home. Services outside the home (a day-care center, for example) qualify if they involve the care of a qualified child who regularly spends at least eight hours a day in the taxpayer's home. Payments to a relative for child care also qualify unless the relative is a dependent of the taxpayer or is the taxpayer's child under the age of

19. No credit is allowed for the cost of an overnight camp. In addition to this tax credit, you may be able to reduce your costs further by choosing a day-care center that bases its fees on parental income or that offers some kind of "scholarship" or other subsidy for parents in financial difficulties.

But it's important to note in connection with day care that the size of your weekly fee is not directly related to quality. Many excellent centers can charge lower fees because they meet their expenses by mounting effective fund-raising events, by lobbying successfully for state and county aid, by soliciting contributions from community charities or local industries, and by using parent volunteers in all but professional positions. Hence, although you should not always choose the least expensive of two or more possibilities, there is no guarantee that the more expensive choice will be the better one.

Some Alternatives

Although a good day-care center may be in many ways the best child-care alternative for most parents, it simply isn't available everywhere. But one of the following arrangements is almost certain to be feasible in virtually any community.

A Parents' Co-op Under this arrangement a group of parents who live close by one another, have different work schedules, and have children of roughly the same ages take turns in supervising the children in their homes, with no money changing hands. Although this plan is unlikely to work out as a long-term, full-time arrangement, it's obviously economical and it can be invaluable as an interim solution until more professional day care becomes available.

It's always possible, of course, that one of the parents—if he works for low wages or if she loses her job—may decide to "go professional" and take care of children for pay, since no state license may be required if the number of children cared for is small. On the other hand, the cooperating group of parents may serve as a nucleus to persuade an employer, a church, or a social agency to establish a full-time center.

Live-in Child Care Although a live-in housekeeper may be affordable by affluent families, her education and experience are not likely to make her suitable as a mother-substitute. Experienced nannies are even more expensive, and they are not available in all parts of the country. And the immigration laws make it prohibitively difficult to import a foreign student willing to exchange child-care for the opportunity to live with an American family. Nevertheless, it is often possible—especially in college or university communities—to find a student willing to take care of your child in return for room, board, and perhaps a small cash allowance.

Although this arrangement doesn't offer the child the group experiences of a day-care center, it can be extremely satisfactory—especially if the student is made to feel part of the family and develops a warm, "older sister" relationship with the child. But the likelihood of success depends on very careful preliminaries (interviewing several candidates and obtaining references from the college and the student's home community) and detailed agreement beforehand on such matters as hours, duties, responsibilities, use of the telephone, television, and other household equipment, and entertaining friends. Unfortunately, a student's college courses, which usually require some daytime attendance, may make her or him unavailable during your working hours.

There should be a clear understanding, too, that the initial two or three weeks of employment are probationary—so that the student can find out whether she can handle the routine and so that you can evaluate not only her reliability and her performance but also your reaction to the loss of privacy that her arrival makes almost inevitable.

Unlicensed Child Care   Because a state license is usually not required for the care of a small number of children (typically, fewer than six), some individuals or couples in communities lacking professional day-care facilities offer child-care services in their own homes. Some desperate parents, viewing this arrangement through rose-colored glasses, envision a kindly, granny-like woman—perhaps a retired schoolteacher—nurturing their child with love, milk, and cookies. Fearful parents, on the other hand, tend to envision a Dickensian slum with half a dozen ill-assorted and unkempt children squabbling on a dirty living room floor in front of a television set.

Although both images are undoubtedly overdrawn, there are some dangers that should not be overlooked. To begin with, because the lack of licensing and the general informality of the arrangement make it very difficult for parents to check on standards of cleanliness, nutrition, and other essentials, your child's chances of picking up a communicable childhood disease may be higher than at a day-care center. Second, since this is usually a one-person operation, that person's unexpected illness can leave you in the lurch. Perhaps more important, because most of the people who offer this kind of child care are elderly and have low incomes, their educational level is unlikely to be very high. As a result their mode of child rearing as well as their language style may be different enough from yours to cause you some concern.

Although your choice may be limited, you can use some of the criteria applicable to day-care centers to evaluate the available small-group care providers so as to get the best possible care for your child.

Flextime Some employers who have not gone so far as to provide or subsidize full-time day care permit the parents of young children to adjust their work schedules so that one parent can be at home whenever child care requires it. And in some occupations—college teaching, for example—a parent may be able to arrange her or his own work schedule to accomplish this without formal permission. In still other situations an employer will offer one job to a couple, with each of them determining their own hours as long as they fulfill the total. None of these plans is sufficiently widespread to allow for systematic evaluation, but it is easy to see how they may retard the professional advancement of participants who miss important meetings or other information because they are at home taking care of the children.

Assessing the Costs Women have entered the work force in large numbers for a variety of reasons. Some work at routine and ungratifying jobs because their incomes are needed to maintain even a minimum standard of living for their family. Others enjoy the opportunity to use their professional training in productive ways. Still others want to become established in a field in which they intend to work when their children grow older.

But the true "cost" of a mother's job includes not only the costs of day care but the other expenses of working—transportation, clothing, and income taxes. It is only after both spouses cooperatively calculate these costs that a decision can be made as to whether her job is worthwhile. Single parents, of course, have less freedom of choice. But in any situation, continuous monitoring is necessary to ensure that your child is getting the best care available.

ALLOWANCES

In most American homes, children know as little about family finances as they do about their parents' sexual practices, but many child-rearing experts don't regard this financial ignorance as blissful. They don't recommend that young children should be invited to share parents' serious financial problems, but they suggest that even young children, no matter what their parents' income level, should be taught that income is limited, that some of it must be saved, and that the rest must be carefully allocated among long-range, "big" items such as cars, refrigerators, and summer vacation trips, daily necessities such as food, clothing, and electricity, and spontaneous "fun" items such as movie tickets and restaurant checks. They need to learn, too, the seemingly self-evident fact that money spent in one category is simply not available for the others.

In the preadolescent years, the basic purpose of an allowance is to teach the child the concept of budgeting and to provide some practice in using money—but there are other ways of accomplishing this long before an allowance becomes necessary. If, on your supermarket trips and other shopping expeditions, you take your child along and encourage him to witness (or even participate in) the choices and decisions that need to be made, he will get at least a preliminary understanding of how money is used and allocated.

The allowance, then, is simply a small-scale transfer of some of this responsibility for decision-making to the child. Thus, if in the course of a shopping trip the child is enchanted by a small toy of some sort, your saying, "Well, do you think it's worth spending your allowance on? I thought you were saving up for a pair of roller skates" may give him second thoughts—about its quality, its durability, and whether he "really" wants it. If, on the other hand, you were to give it to him unconditionally and pay for it yourself, the child is unlikely to develop the consumer skills that will prove beneficial later in life.

The age at which an allowance should begin can't be specified precisely. Obviously it's not necessary until the child is exposed to opportunities to buy things and has some discretion about what to buy. But if, for example, the child takes lunch money to school, you might consider giving her a small sum over and above the lunch charge that she can spend on "anything she likes"—with the clear understanding that the lunch money is to be spent exclusively for the school lunch.

As the child grows older, and as she and her peers range over a territory that includes shopping malls and department stores, both her "needs" and her opportunities for meeting them will expand, and her allowance should be raised proportionately. At this stage the allowance can teach her to make choices among small, "impulse" items, such as a new lipstick, larger ones, such as a "top forty" tape cassette, and really big ones, such as a bicycle or a stereo, which require an accumulation of many weeks of allowances. Inevitably, she will make mistakes, but such mistakes are an essential part of her consumer education.

As the child grows older, peer group pressure increases rapidly and may express itself either as "All the other kids have a————. Why can't I?" or as "We must be very poor, because all the other kids get twice as much allowance as I do." It's difficult to know how to respond to such pleas. On the one hand, parents need to empathize with the agony of children who feel that they are outsiders or "different." On the other hand, children need to be taught to endure nonconformity if it has a rational basis that can be explained to them in terms that they can understand.

Because the allowance provides the child with tangible evidence of your love and trust, it's not a good idea to withhold or suspend it as a punishment for misbehavior, and it should probably carry no restrictions ("You can't use it to buy Cokes!"). Part of a child's development involves experimenting with "forbidden" items, and your restrictions may simply make the forbidden more attractive. Of course, if your child persistently misspends the allowance, you will need to take some action, but suspending the allowance is unlikely to be the most effective.

Children are almost certain to lose money occasionally. This, too, is part of the learning process and, although the parents need not feel obligated to replace the loss, they should not add to it with a scolding. More serious in some neighborhoods is the danger that the child will be "shaken down" by bigger or older classmates. You can teach the child to reduce this danger by not flaunting his money or talking about it, but it is even more important to persuade him that in a confrontation he should give up the money rather than attempt resistance. The danger that this "cowardice" will make him an easy victim in the future can be dealt with in other ways—through the school authorities or the police. The danger from resistance is a far greater threat.

PLAYTHINGS AND OTHER GIFTS

Although toys can range in price from a 79¢ water pistol or a set of jacks to a $300 bicycle or a $1,000 computer, planning for them on your budget is far less important than thinking about their purpose and their appropriateness for the child's age and interests. Once you have clearly in mind what kind of toys you want and why you want them, you'll be able to pass with relative safety through the mine-fields of overpriced plastic junk (batteries not included) displayed in discount department stores and in pre-Christmas television commercials and end up with something that you will give and the child will receive with pleasure.

"Educational Toys"

The label "educational" does not have much meaning when applied to toys, since almost everything the child plays with is educational in one way or another, and often the educational value is unrelated to price. The two-year-old who plays randomly on the kitchen floor with pots and pans, the cores of the paper towel rolls, and a few plastic utensils is likely to learn more about shapes, sizes, textures, weight, noise, and color than she would from an "educational" mobile hung over her crib. The five-year-old who transforms a $4 "car" made of a block of maple with a wheel at each corner into an ambulance, a sports car, an interstate freight carrier, or a family sedan is learning to exercise his imagination far more actively than his playmate who owns a $50 exquisitely detailed scale model of a racing car or an eighteen-wheeler.

The ten-year-old who assembles a not-too-difficult model ship or plane learns the rewards of patience and exacting craftsmanship, which he could not possibly learn from hours of play with a shoot-'em-down video or computer game. The child who can become engrossed in a book—and motivated to read others—is certain to develop more verbal skills than the child who spends the same amount of time fiddling with a joystick or a computer keyboard.

Toys teach not only specific skills but also broad values. Because our society stresses competitiveness, most toys and games stress competition and end with a winner and a loser. You may feel, of course, that your child needs to learn how to win and lose gracefully (although no competitive game guarantees this outcome). On the other hand, if you'd like your child to develop social competence and skill in cooperation, you might choose a construction set, a sandbox, or a dollhouse, all of which encourage cooperative play with siblings, friends, and neighbors.

Still more broadly, toys reflect society's general concern either with production or with consumption. Fifty years ago, because our society was focused on production, the popular toys were construction sets, chemistry sets, toy stoves and cooking utensils, and other items that motivated children to "make" something. Today, with society's emphasis having shifted to consumption, the most popular toys teach children to become consumers. Model cars turn five-year-olds into sophisticated automobile enthusiasts, just as Barbie™ dolls introduce them to the broad market of clothing and coiffures. Nevertheless, parents still have a choice between "production" toys and "consumption" toys.

Parents whose child shows interest in a "production" activity, or who want to encourage the child's participation in their own hobbies—woodworking, for example, or sewing or music or writing—often buy the child "toy" carpenter's tools, sewing machines, instruments, or typewriters. These are almost always so inferior to the real thing that they tend to discourage the child—and often they are just as expensive as a good secondhand model of the real thing. To satisfy or stimulate a budding interest, consider buying, as the child's "very own," a good but manageable plane or saw, a secondhand sewing machine, an electronic keyboard or a downsized violin, or one of the thousands of secondhand typewriters that have been replaced in recent years by word processors. These "grown-up" devices that "really work" can give the child a genuine sense of participation and encourage him to take them seriously.

Although all toys are educational, the most effective are those that provide spontaneous fun and are not merely sugar-coated pills. The recent emphasis on "educational" toys that develop skill with letters and numbers and provide the child with "challenge"—all with the implicit or explicit promise of giving him a competitive advantage when he enters school—has resulted in a proliferation of toys that provide too much challenge or that don't offer much fun even when the child meets their challenge. To provide relief from all these earnest efforts at "improvement," the child should be allowed toys that simply promote "noneducational" high-spirited play—a frisbee, a water pistol, a kite, a dartboard.

The Timing of Toys

The manufacturers' age guidelines—the "Not suitable for children under age 5" warnings that appear on the carton—usually relate to safety rather than to the child's capacity to enjoy them, and they need not be taken seriously when judging age-appropriateness of the toy. On the other hand, many parents, eager to push their child's development, tend to buy toys and games that are clearly too advanced: a chess set for a three-year-old, or a two-wheeled bicycle for a five-year-old. The notion that "he'll grow into it" won't always correct this mistake, because a child's first experience with a toy or game that he finds "too hard" or frightening may well turn him against it permanently.

Parents—and especially grandparents—can make another kind of "timing" mistake by assuming that their own favorite childhood toy is certain to enchant the recipient too. Fashions in toys change, as does their technology, and the doll or the model steam engine you loved in your own childhood may elicit from your child a blank stare rather than the squeals of delight and gratitude that you anticipated.

The timing of gifts—in the sense of *when* they should be given—can create some friction between spouses because there are two views on this, neither necessarily correct. Some parents believe that Christmas or Chanukah and birthdays are the most appropriate occasions for gifts and that at these festive times the child should be almost overwhelmed with them. Other parents argue that this practice does, indeed, overwhelm the child and may prevent her from appreciating any one gift. These parents prefer to make gifts spontaneously—when the child expresses a desire or "need" for some specific thing (e.g., a tennis racket) or simply as a generous impulse unrelated to a particular occasion.

Perhaps the best policy is to make small, inexpensive gifts spontaneously but to reserve "big" presents—a complete ski outfit, for example, or an expensive camera—for special occasions. Forcing a child to wait for something he wants very much may strike you as cruel, but it can teach him a trait that may serve him well in later life: sociologists call it "the ability to defer gratification"; the rest of us call it the ability to tolerate frustration with patience and grace.

This policy may seem inconvenient if the child wants a pair of skis and her birthday falls in July, but you can solve the problem comfortably by giving her on her birthday an attractively lettered I.O.U. for a pair of skis to be delivered shortly before the season opens. The I.O.U. offers you the opportunity to shop at pre-season sales, and it's especially useful if the present is intended as a surprise but needs to be custom-fitted, or if the child would like to choose among several makes and models.

A Matter of Taste

Conflict between parent and child often arises because the child desperately wants as a gift something that the parent doesn't approve of—an unsuitable piece of clothing, a sweatshirt lettered with a message that's in questionable taste, a personal television set or telephone. This is a difficult situation because, as you may recall from your own childhood, peer pressure and the need to conform can be excruciating; on the other hand, you have the right to insist on certain standards of appearance and to prohibit certain kinds of behavior or use of leisure time.

Some parents solve this problem with a flat "If you want it, you'll have to buy it with your own money," but this simply shirks parental responsibility. It may be sensible in the case of a personal telephone line—especially if such a purchase ends the child's monopoly of the family phone—but if you are firmly convinced that excessive television viewing will interfere with your child's school work, whether a personal television set is bought with her money or yours is irrelevant.

LESSONS: MUSIC, DANCE, AND OTHER PERFORMING ARTS

Whether or not you and your child will get pleasure and value from lessons in music, dance, figure skating, or some other performing art depends less on the "talent" your child may have than on your reasons for proposing the lessons in the first place. There are two bad reasons and three good ones.

Motivations—Bad and Good

The worst reason—but one that is shared by many parents—is the hope or expectation that in a decade or two you will be sitting proudly in the front row at Carnegie Hall or Lincoln Center and watching your child perform on stage. Statistically the probability of this is far lower than your chances of winning a million dollars in the state lottery, but, as in the case of the lottery, these odds don't discourage a good many parents. Of course, a losing lottery ticket can be thrown away and forgotten. But losing this career lottery can cost both you and your child years of unhappiness and frustration.

Talent is, of course, essential for star performance, but it's not enough. Most world-famous performers—especially in music—began at the age of four or five under powerful and *informed* parental pressure and devoted themselves single-mindedly to full-time lessons and practice for the rest of their lives. (The starting age for prima ballerinas is about nine, and the training just as stressful.) And of the many thousands of young people who started out on these careers, only a handful achieve international standing. Some of the also-rans hold chairs in symphony orchestras, play minor roles in major performances, or have turned to teaching, either in schools or privately. And so, even if your child has talent—and this is very difficult to measure—your hopes for his or her future celebrity are most unlikely to be fulfilled.

A second bad reason involves keeping up with the Joneses—that is, buying a piano and forcing lessons on your child simply because your friends and neighbors are all doing this or because you feel that your income level makes it the appropriate thing for you to do. People who buy themselves this kind of status symbol usually wind up with an unused piano and a child who is permanently alienated from music that does not emanate from a boombox.

But there are three good reasons that make lessons very well worthwhile and if these motivate you, your child is likely to avoid frustration and enjoy several kinds of pleasure. To begin with, it is almost impossible to enjoy fully any art or craft—music, dance, painting, or even a piece of fine cabinetwork—if one has not had some active, firsthand experience with it oneself. Many of us with no formal training in music can, of course, get pleasure from a harpsichord recital or a Beethoven quartet. But our pleasure is almost certain to be less keen than that of the listener who has played the harpsichord (or the piano) or who has studied enough theory and harmony to understand exactly what Beethoven was doing.

The same is true, of course, of any spectator activity: one can fully appreciate a tennis match or a sailing race or a ballet only if one has tried to do—even very amateurishly—what the experts we are watching do. And so, even if your child never becomes more than a mediocre amateur violinist or pianist, the training will sharpen her or his appreciation of music for the rest of her or his life.

But the child who progresses even slightly beyond the mediocre-ama-teur level is likely to find that musical skill becomes a valuable social asset. Joining a school orchestra or a school band is a fine way to make friends, and so is playing informally at parties and other gatherings. Despite the popularity of cassettes and compact discs, music made by a group gathered around a piano or a guitar still has infinitely more appeal than the canned versions—both to the participants and to the listeners.

The third—and probably most important—advantage of lessons reaches far beyond the performance of music or dance itself. Actually, what the long hours of difficult and sometimes tedious practice teach the student is not only that an excellent level of performance is not reached easily or quickly and that absolute perfection is almost unattainable but that persistence and hard work do result in very rewarding improvements and eventual mastery. This realization, which is almost essential for success in any endeavor, may serve your child well long after the music lessons have been abandoned.

Keeping the Initial Investment Low

Like sex education, music lessons are likely to be most successful if they are asked for by the child rather than imposed by the parent. But, of course, you can do much to stimulate your child's interest by giving him good musical toys and cassettes and exposing him to music at home by singing songs and nursery rhymes, playing your own cassettes or CDs, and taking him to concerts and other public performances fairly early in life. But even when it seems strong, a child's interest may be short-lived, and so it's a good idea to keep your investment—both in instruments and in lessons—as low as you can until his initial interest is reinforced by actual experience.

How low you can keep it depends to a large extent on your local school. In many of the more affluent public school systems, the music programs include group lessons and even provide the students with instruments on long-term loan. And some university extension divisions offer introductory parent-and-child courses in recorder, guitar, and other popular instruments at nominal cost. Such lessons may not satisfy your child for very long if his enthusiasm flourishes, but they are more than adequate to determine whether his interest is likely to persist, and, unlike some private teachers, the people who teach them are not apt to exaggerate your child's ability simply to retain him as a long-term student.

If your local school doesn't offer instruction, you may be able to find a private music school that is relatively inexpensive. And the music departments of most colleges and universities can usually recommend graduate students who are preparing for a career as music teachers.

Except for graduate students, don't hire a music teacher who is willing to come to your home for lessons. Good teachers, like most doctors, place too high a value on their time to make house calls. And don't try to economize by hiring as a teacher the older child of a friend or neighbor who plays an instrument but has had no experience in teaching. Music teaching is a profession, and even talented amateurs don't know how to practice it.

Your investment will be low, too, if you can persuade your child to begin with an inexpensive instrument (a perfectly adequate basic recorder, which is an excellent instrument for beginners, costs about $10) or by renting instead of buying. If this turns out to be impractical, hunt for a secondhand instrument. In most communities the classified advertising columns are crowded with offers of good second-hand instruments in which the original owner has lost interest.

Of course, some secondhand instruments may be unplayable and beyond repair. It's not wise to buy a used piano before having it checked by a tuner—or any other instrument without having it checked by a teacher or a very competent player. But most such instruments can be refurbished or repaired for far less than the cost of a new one.

It's important to distinguish between the *condition* of an instrument and its *quality*. Nobody can learn to play on an instrument that's in poor condition—for example, a piano that can't be kept in tune for more than a couple of days—but quality does not become important for many years. James Galway may feel that he plays at his best on a solid-gold flute. But your child can do quite well for many years on a used one that costs you $200. And, of course, if he falls in love with the flute, what better birthday present can you give him than a new one—for perhaps $800?

The Other Performing Arts

Thus far we've dealt mainly with music lessons—because this is what parents are most likely to want for their children—but much of what we've said applies to the other performing arts.

Dance—modern, classical, or popular—presents a special problem, because so many mothers have professional aspirations for their daughters and because so few professionally qualified teachers are available in any but the half-dozen largest cities. Training under a competent teacher can give a student not only a "professional" appreciation of ballet performances but also a lifelong grace of posture and movement—but it is *not* likely to result in a professional career. Training under one of the numerous incompetents who are exploiting the huge demand and who use frequent recitals as a form of advertising will give the student little. The polite applause at her recital performance may give your daughter an inflated notion of her ability, which in turn, may increase her frustration at her almost inevitable failure to turn dance into a career.

You or Your Child?

As we've noted earlier, lessons in any performing art are likely to be most effective when the child expresses a spontaneous interest in them or when she responds happily to the parent who proposes them. All too often, however, lessons are urged or forced on the child because they satisfy some need of the parent. The parent who had a generally deprived childhood may want to give his child "all the advantages I myself never had." The parent who feels that his or her own career is generally undistinguished may seek vicarious status through forcing his child to take figure-skating lessons—not for the joy of figure skating but in the hope that she will win the national championship. If the child does not respond to these pressures—or if the response is grudging and reluctant—neither the child nor the parent is likely to be enriched by the process.

SUMMER CAMP

If you regard summer camp as an unnecessary luxury, you may be overlooking some of its very real values for you and for your child. Sending the child to camp can give you and your spouse not only the freedom to do "grown-up" things but also uninterrupted time together—a commodity especially precious if you both work. And many children find camp a far better place than school for learning new skills and making new friends.

But summer camps are not inexpensive. The weekly fee at a traditional fun-and-games camp can run to more than $350, and specialized camps (for weight loss, for example, or computer programming) charge as much as $800. These camps generally have a minimum session of four weeks. On the other hand, camps run by such nonprofit organizations as the Boy Scouts or the YMCA cost about $300 a week and offer shorter sessions.

The cost of summer camp, however, is not directly related to the "value received"—by both you and your child. In fact, a recent survey concluded that campers attending the least expensive camps were just as happy with their experiences as those attending the most expensive—although, admittedly, their expectations may have differed. Hence, knowing what kind of camp you and your child want, and shopping for it carefully several months ahead of time, is likely to get you better value than spending a lot of money on the assumption that "you get what you pay for."

There are a couple of ways, however, in which you can reduce your costs. First, because summer camp is regarded as an "extra" rather than a routine parental expense, camp fees can be paid out of the child's custodial account (see p. 55) instead of out of your own pocket. In addition, if both you and your spouse earn income, the camp fees for a traditional recreational day camp (but not for one with specialized programs in, for example, basketball or computer operation) can be included in the child-care tax credit on your income tax return (see pp. 68–69).

But cost is rarely the main issue. Far more important is the willingness of your child to go to camp at all. Every child is likely to demonstrate some anxiety about being away from home, but this can usually be overcome with patience and understanding. On the other hand, simply incarcerating a child in an unfamiliar camp against his will may free you to go off on a junket to Europe but may present you with serious problems when you return.

Day Camps

One way to allay a child's separation anxiety is to begin with one season of day camp so that he can experience some of the pleasures of camping without giving up the security of living at home. Although day camping doesn't offer the parents a great deal of personal freedom, it costs much less than a residential camp and it can diminish if not demolish the child's worries about going off to a regular camp next year.

Like conventional away-from-home camps, day camps vary widely in quality and cost. Because operating a day camp requires little or no capital investment, some of them consist of little more than a station wagon manned by inexperienced college students who transport the campers to a public park for a day of athletics and games. For this reason, you ought to investigate references with respect to the camp's past performance (especially reliability and punctuality of pick-up and delivery) and check carefully on the camp's current health and liability insurance coverage as well as its plans and facilities for rainy-day activities. Many of the criteria we'll list later in this chapter can be used to separate the better from the worse.

What Type of Camp?

Once the child is receptive—or at least not resistant—to the prospect of going off to camp, the next decision usually involves the camp program. In general, camps fall into two categories: traditional and specialized. The program at the traditional camp includes a range of familiar outdoor and indoor activities—competitive sports, swimming, nature study, hiking, field trips, arts and crafts, games, and so on. The special-purpose camp includes some of these activities but devotes most of its schedule to its specialty: sailing, riding, computer programming, music, art, marine biology, survival skills, soccer, tennis. Some special-ized camps offer remedial programs for a specific group of children—those who are overweight or who are academic underachievers.

The specialized camp may appeal to a child, because its focus on an existing interest or enthusiasm may reduce his anxiety about being away from home and build his self-confidence in relationships with fellow campers. The young computer hacker, for example, may look forward not only to learning more about his hobby but also to showing off his current expertise to his bunk mates. But these special-purpose camps usually appeal to older children who, presumably, have spent time away from home before.

The special-purpose camp can, however, have several disadvantages. To begin with, it almost inevitably costs more—sometimes significantly more—than the traditional camp. Moreover, it may not accomplish its advertised purpose. Many of the children who attend weight-reduction camps, for example, revert to their original weight shortly after they return home.

In addition, some of these camps have a no-nonsense, achievement-centered atmosphere that differs little from what the child experiences at school. At best, they are likely to intensify an existing interest instead of introducing the child to a broad range of new activities and interests. For this reason they may appeal to parents who continuously strive to push the child toward high achievement or who feel that a demonstrable improvement in tennis or reading skill is tangible evidence that they've got their money's worth.

The traditional unspecialized camp, on the other hand, can, at its best, offer the child an environment quite different from the classroom and encourage him to develop new interests and enthusiasms through a leisurely, noncompetitive exploration of the unfamiliar. Certainly the urban child is likely to learn more at camp by hiking a mountain trail or visiting a salmon hatchery than by spending much of the day hunched over a computer keyboard or trying to come about in a sailboat three seconds faster than he did five minutes earlier.

Choosing a Camp

If cost is a major consideration, you might look first at the camps operated by the Boy Scouts and Girl Scouts, the Camp Fire Girls, the YMCA and YWCA, the Salvation Army, and some local church groups. Although they vary widely in quality and facilities both within each of the sponsoring groups and among them, these not-for-profit camps in general are likely to be somewhat more spartan in terms of meals, accommodations, and equipment than their more expensive privately operated counterparts. But this kind of wholesome simplicity may appeal to your child, and the prospect of having as tent mates local youngsters he already knows may make him feel more comfortable about being away from home.

Reliable information about the thousands of privately operated camps is hard to come by, because most of the published directories use unverified information provided by the camps themselves and because camp referral services collect commissions from the camps they list. The one official accrediting organization, the American Camping Association, publishes formal standards, but its inspection of the accredited camps is not frequent, and it is quite possible that a number of good camps choose not to join its membership. The camps that it accredits are listed in *The Guide to Accredited Camps* (American Camping Association, P.O. Box 101, Bradford Woods, Martinsville, IN 46151), which also includes tips on choosing the right camp and comparing costs. Another biennial directory, *The Guide to Summer Camps and Summer Schools* (Porter Sargent Publishers, Inc., 11 Beacon St., Boston, MA 02108), may be useful if you are looking for a specialized camp, although the information it contains is provided by the camps themselves.

Sheldon Silver and Jeremy Solomon's *The Smart Parents' Guide to Summer Camps* (Farrar Straus & Giroux, 1991) offers some useful guidance on the choice of a camp, but there is no indication of the source of the camp data, and the rates quoted are likely to be outdated. Richard C. Smith and Michael Kimball's *Choosing the Right Camp* (Times Books, 1993) is another useful source.

In response to your request for information, some camps will send you luxuriously printed brochures or video cassettes, others will invite you to a slideshow, and still others will make an appointment for a visit to your home. Bear in mind, however, that camps rely heavily on repeat business and on word-of-mouth recommendations and, hence, the better the camp, the less its need for expensive and high-pressure advertising. Your best source of information is likely to be personal acquaintances who have sent children to camp or, lacking that, a list of parents (not a selected few "satisfied customers") provided by the camps in which you are interested. If, however, you attend a recruiting meeting or request a private, at-home presentation, you might try to get specific answers to some of the following questions:

Who Is the Director? Because the camp director sets the tone of the entire operation, the basic question is whether he or she is a professional or simply an entrepreneur. This distinction is sometimes difficult to make, but a personal interview is far more reliable than a printed list of credentials. Many directors are certified teachers or professionals licensed in some area of child development. But this in itself is no guarantee of a dedication to children. Many teachers see the operation of a summer camp as nothing more than a way of supplementing their income, and to them the bottom line may be far more important than the quality of the program. On the other hand, some teacher-directors regard their annual camp experience as the most satisfying part of their year—professionally and personally though not necessarily financially.

Find out, too, whether the director takes an active part in the daily program. Some directors do; others function as largely absentee owners of two or more camps.

What's the Program Like? If the camp program is specialized, ask questions about the equipment. (How many computers will be shared by how many campers? Is sailing taught individually or on a group basis? Do campers have access to equipment during their free time?)

Whether the camp is specialized or traditional, try to get a feeling about the program. Is it highly structured, or do campers have free time to do what they like? (And ask yourself which of these is more suitable for your child.) Are any of the activities compulsory? Do the activities emphasize competitiveness or cooperation? What happens when bad weather cancels a planned activity? And are the campers monitored about writing letters to parents? Is there adequate medical supervision by a staff doctor or a local practitioner? And are campers who require special diets carefully supervised?

What about the Staff? What is the ratio of campers to counselors? And what are the counselors like? The American Camping Association requires accredited camps to enroll no more than five to eight campers per counselor, depending on the age of the campers. It specifies, also, that at least 80% of the counselors must be be over the age of 18 and at least 20% have college degrees.

Ask also about the qualifications of the counselors and other staff members. How many of the swimming instructors have Red Cross certificates? Are the tennis instructors qualified tournament participants or simply enthusiastic amateurs? Does the camp employ a registered nurse and a licensed dietitian?

Money Matters Inquire, too, about the refund policy if your child should have to withdraw before the end of the season. Find out whether you can sign up for only half the season and then commit yourself for the second half if the child is happy with his experience. And, to avoid unpleasant surprises, ask about extra fees for special services or activities. Check also on the camp's health and liability insurance coverage should your child be injured on a field trip or in the course of regular activities.

Who's Going to Camp?

Throughout the regular school year, what goes on in your child's daily classes is determined largely by his teacher, the principal, and the board of education—and not by you. This may frustrate you at times—if, for example, you feel that his teacher's expectations of him are too low—

but it also protects your child against your imposing your own expectations and pressures—which just possibly may be too high. In choosing a camp, on the other hand, you are free to find one whose program fits closely to your own ideas and standards. But if you make this choice without consulting the child, he no longer has this protection and may have a very unhappy summer.

Summer is, after all, a time for vacation fun, and camp is a place that presumably can provide more fun than the child can have alone. Obviously, part of the fun will stem from learning new skills and having new experiences, but camp should not be looked upon as a place to "improve" the child. Survival camps which require campers to face dangers and overcome difficulties may produce in some campers the "self-confidence" they promise, but in others they may produce terror and humiliation. Camps that offer weight-reduction may or may not return your child a few pounds lighter, but whether they give her a happy, carefree summer is a very different question.

YOUR CHILD'S SCHOOLING—
PUBLIC OR PRIVATE?

The alternative of sending your child to a private school may occur to you either because you're unhappy with the local public school or because your child is having learning or behavioral difficulties that his current teachers seem unable to resolve. But a sound decision is not easy to reach, because it involves a number of factors: your motivations and your income, your spouse's opinion, your child's specific abilities, deficiencies, and preferences, and the kinds of public and private schools available to you.

These factors are so various, and they combine in so many ways, that a simple, clear-cut answer that is applicable to all children in all situations is obviously impossible. But although the issue of public vs. private schooling is an individual one, it also has powerful political, social, and emotional overtones. For this reason, before seeking a yes-or-no answer to your own question, you may find it useful to look at the issue from a broad perspective. This overall view may, in fact, change some of your current thinking.

What's Available

Although the United States is among the world's leaders in its dedication to universal public education, private schools have existed since the earliest times—to serve some of the same purposes they serve today.

A great many, if not most, of the nation's private schools are church-affiliated. Because of the constitutional separation of church and state, American public schools are more or less secular, and parents who want a school to reinforce the religious values that their children learn at home may prefer a private institution, whether it be a Catholic parochial school, a Hebrew yeshiva, a Quaker school, or one operated by some other religious group.

Not all religious or church-affiliated schools restrict their admissions to the children of adherents, not all of them conduct a strong program of religious indoctrination, and some of them attract students by means of high academic standards and an enriched curriculum rather than a religious orientation. Nevertheless, many private schools are populated largely if not exclusively by students of the same religion.

But social status also plays a part in parental decisions. Because the public schools are open to all children, some parents of high social status are concerned about protecting their children from classroom and playground contact with "the lower orders"—especially if these "undesirable" children belong to minority groups. The famous New England prep schools originally admitted only "old money" white Anglo-Saxon Protestants and, although in recent years they have significantly relaxed their admission requirements as to income level and racial and ethnic background, they still retain an "upper class" atmosphere and style that makes them irresistibly attractive to parents who strive to maintain or improve their own social standing.

Capitalizing on the same concerns of parents but catering to a rather different social level, a number of "white Christian academies" sprang up in the South immediately after the 1954 Supreme Court school desegregation decision. These were intended to provide worried parents with an alternative to desegregated classrooms.

Some private schools have been established to meet the needs of "exceptional" children—a term that includes children with mental retardation, emotional disturbance, behavioral problems, and learning difficulties as well as those who show signs of intellectual or artistic promise. This group includes military academies, designed to instill "discipline" in disobedient boys; schools that provide custodial settings for the mentally retarded; specialized institutions that offer therapy as well as special education to children who are blind, deaf, emotionally disturbed, or brain-damaged; schools offering remedial programs for "underachievers"; and schools providing enriched programs designed to challenge the intellectually gifted.

Still another group of private schools caters to a different kind of "special" student—the budding musician, artist, or ballet dancer. These provide individual and group instruction in the student's field of interest in addition to the traditional college-preparatory academic courses.

Pros and Cons

Given the wide variety of purposes served by private schools, it would not be surprising if one of them struck you as attractive for your own child. But the issue of private vs. public schooling has aroused heated controversy among both professional educators and parents, and a brief look at the arguments presented by each side may influence some of your own thinking.

Uniformity or Variety? Those in favor of private schooling argue that individual children have different needs, that the public schools, with their large classes, are too homogeneous to cater to all these needs, and that parents have the right to choose from a broader "menu" of educational offerings. But their opponents point out that the private schools not only drain off many of the better students from the public schools but also dilute public support and participation from their parents (who may be well educated, affluent, highly sophisticated, and politically effective) and that both the "brain drain" and the loss of support prevent the public schools from improving. These opponents point to a number of localities in which parents who could afford private schooling for their children opted against it, directed their efforts toward upgrading the local public system, and produced significant improvements that benefited all children.

The "religion" issue is also not altogether simple. Presumably parents have the right to instill their children with their own religious beliefs—and, in fact, in recent years there has been growing concern over the alleged failure of the public schools to teach moral values and ethical behavior. But many of the people who are concerned about the need for teaching moral values feel that parental responsibility includes an obligation to prepare children for life in an increasingly secular and socially heterogeneous society. If, they argue, education in a religious school shelters children from contact with a wide variety of students, ideas, and value systems, or if it provides them with a restricted education in the sciences, the children may find themselves handicapped in terms of their further education and future careers.

Elitism, Social and Academic The "social" exclusivity of the private school has also been open to argument and challenge. Virtually all parents prefer that their children associate with others of the same (or higher) social status, and this preference often determines their choice of neighborhood and generates their opposition to busing programs intended to produce integrated classes. This is why, faced with the prospect of their child's being bused out of their neighborhood to an integrated school, many parents opt for the private school. But because they are reluctant to acknowledge their social prejudices, most of them justify their decision on the grounds that the private school's superior academic program will improve their child's prospects of admission to a highly selective college.

Superficially this looks like a sound argument, because their admissions statistics indicate that such colleges as Harvard, Yale, and Princeton show a marked preference for private school graduates. But a closer look at these statistics raises some questions: Are the preppies admitted because of their schooling, or are they superior students who might have gained admission even had they attended public schools? If an unmotivated and not-very-bright student manages to gain admission to a private school, is he or she likely to be admitted by a high-prestige (and therefore highly selective) college?

The Academic Realities A comparison of the academic performance of private and public school graduates at the college level raises further questions. For the first year or so, the private school students earn better grades—but then they are outstripped by their public school classmates. Does the early difference stem from the private school graduates' better preparation in reading, writing, and research skills? Or is it due simply to the fact that public school graduates have not had prior experience in living away from home and that their new freedom (or their homesickness) interferes with their studies?

Even if the Ivy League seems to favor private school graduates, it is important to note that these students must meet the same admissions criteria as their public school competitors and that favoritism between the two groups will occur only when "all other things are equal"—in this case, the quality of the students' high school records and perhaps their SAT scores. This point is especially important because, during the period of economic prosperity between 1950 and 1990, a number of private schools sprang up which offer socially ambitious but unsophisticated parents a "reasonable facsimile" of Exeter, Andover, Groton, Choate, and the few other schools that have earned stellar reputations. But both the academic standards of these schools and the future careers of their graduates lead some critics to regard the facsimile as rather less than reasonable.

Even the social exclusivity of the private preparatory school has come under fire on the grounds that its students are deprived of social experience with classmates whose social status is very different from their own. In recent years, the genuinely "upper class" prep schools, apparently recognizing the disadvantages of a single-class student body, have deliberately broadened their student population by offering scholarships and other inducements to members of minorities and other students who could not afford the tuition and who, in past years, would have been rejected even if they could. On the other hand, the "reasonable facsimile" type of prep school provides little social cachet to begin with, since its population is likely to consist almost exclusively of the children of the socially ambitious rather than the socially distinguished.

The Quality of Teaching   Many advocates of the private preparatory school argue that these institutions have better teaching staffs than the public schools because they are exempt from the bureaucratic regulations that require the public schools to employ only teachers who are "certificated" by the state department of education, no matter how dreary or uninspired they may be in the classroom. Thus, the defenders imply that every private school class is taught by a male or female counterpart of Mr. Chips.

This notion is likely to appeal strongly to parents who are disappointed with the professional competence or the personality of their child's public school teachers. But such parents may be equally disappointed with the private school alternative. It is true, of course, that the state systems of public school teacher certification provide only that the teacher has passed certain education courses, and not that he or she is an educated, inspiring, or even minimally interesting person. But freedom from these requirements is no guarantee of excellence. True, some private school teachers are legendary, but such teachers can also be found in the public system. And, if the rate of teacher turnover is any indication, the number of "inspired" but unstable and basically incompetent teachers may be higher in the private schools than in the public.

Schools for the Handicapped   Special private schools for physically, mentally, or emotionally handicapped students have also been subjected to critical scrutiny. Because many parents of such children are understandably desperate, and because both medical and educational resources are often either unavailable or unresponsive to their child's needs, a number of private institutions have sprung up that offer "special" treatments that are no more effective than the quack cures offered to desperate terminally ill cancer patients.

There are, of course, many thoroughly legitimate institutions of this type, and a few decades ago they were an invaluable (though very expensive) resource for beleaguered parents, but two recent developments may have diminished their value. To begin with, research has demonstrated increasingly that "mainstreaming" the handicapped child—that is, placing him in a regular classroom, encouraging him to associate with nonhandicapped classmates, and challenging him with the usual program—is far more effective in promoting both his social and his intellectual development than segregating him with other disabled children in the hope of making him feel more comfortable. Obviously, not every disabled child can be successfully mainstreamed, but many experts believe that parents are more likely to underestimate than overestimate their child's potentials.

Perhaps more important, Public Law 94-142, passed by Congress in 1975, requires the states to identify and evaluate all students who need special education and to provide in writing an educational plan and an individualized instruction program developed jointly by the school, the parents, and, if possible, the child himself. The specialized instruction that the schools must provide includes instruction in the home, a hospital, or an institution, as well as necessary transportation. If the public school cannot provide the necessary facilities, the child must be placed in or referred to a private school at no cost to the parents. Parents of a handicapped child should be in touch with the school authorities before the child's third birthday, because the law requires the state to begin educating handicapped children by age three.

Although some states have been slow to respond to these rulings, recent court decisions have reinforced the principle that the state is responsible for educating *all* children and not only those who have tested within normal physical and mental limits. As a consequence, public school programs for exceptional children are proliferating everywhere, and hard-pressed parents are saving the considerable costs of private schooling. In many communities, parents of handicapped children have banded together to persuade the public education authorities to provide their children with facilities to which the courts have ruled that they are entitled.

The "Problem" Child For the child with academic or behavior problems a private school may be the solution, or it may not. To begin with, it's not always easy to determine whether the child has a genuine problem or whether the "problem" is caused by unrealistic expectations of the parents. Some parents who themselves have achieved outstanding school records are understandably unhappy if their child's school work is perfectly satisfactory but not as outstanding as they would like. Some parents who are socially hyperactive regard their child as socially maladjusted simply because he sometimes prefers to do things by himself rather than with a crowd of friends. In short, some parents see problems simply because they have not produced a clone, even though, in fact, their child is functioning normally.

But there is a further problem. Suppose the child is sent to a private school and shows a marked improvement in grades or behavior. Can this improvement be attributed to the private school or simply to the passage of time and to the change of environment that would have occurred even in the public school? Many, if not most, academic problems tend to be temporary—a matter of the child's growth stage, or his dislike (sometimes justified) of a particular teacher, or the peer group in which he finds himself. True, sending him to a private school will change some of these factors. But so will the passage of time if he remains in the public school. The only way to evaluate a private school for your own child would be to keep him in both schools at the same time—and this is obviously impossible.

The "Gifted" Child The private school for children who are "gifted"—intellectually, musically, artistically—has enjoyed enthusiastic praise, not only from some of its alumni and their parents but also from prominent figures in the arts and sciences. But it has also been criticized on a number of grounds: that its elitism deprives students of contact and experience with "ordinary" peers and that it may develop in its students an exaggerated and unjustified level of self-esteem. In addition, the schools that specialize in the arts have been accused of giving students an inflated notion of their talent and neglecting the academic preparation necessary for college admission, which these days is necessary even for the artistically gifted and especially for those whose talents fall short of their ambitions.

An Inferior Local School System As the table on page 94 indicates, not all states can afford the same kind of school system, and, because schools are funded very largely by local taxes, in some states the differences between adjacent communities are even more dramatic than the differences between states. Although the relationship between per-student expenditures and educational excellence is not perfect (the schools in Alaska, for example, probably spend more money on heating fuel than on microscopes for the advanced biology class) it does tell us something. If you are unhappy with the quality of the local public schools, it may be that you have chosen to live, because of your job situation or the lure of low tax rates, in a community that can't or won't spend enough money to provide good schooling.

But here, too, the public school systems in a number of states provide this kind of special schooling. The City of New York, for example, supports high schools that specialize in the training of future scientists, mathematicians, artists, actors, and musicians, as well as the generally gifted. North Carolina's High School of Performing Arts is a publicly supported boarding school. And Boston's Latin Grammar School offers a stimulating program for intellectually promising students. These tax-supported institutions provide many of the advantages of a private school at little or no cost to the parents.

Not all communities support specialized schools, but virtually every public school of any size tends to segregate its pupils into two or three categories based on academic proficiency. Although this kind of intellectual segregation has been accused, like the private schools, of producing elitism and inflated self-esteem, it has the advantage of costing nothing. If your child seems bored with his daily classes, or if you think that the local school program isn't stimulating him, it's a good idea, before you decide to send him to a private school, to find out whether he has been misclassified, or whether he could be skipped a grade. Conceivably such a move could eliminate the need for a private school altogether.

Reaching a Decision

Although this overview may have prompted you to think further—and perhaps to change your mind—about certain issues, your decision is likely to be influenced most strongly by your personal situation: where you live (and hence the kind of public schooling available) and what special problems your child seems to present (over- or underachievement, social isolation, behavior difficulties, physical or mental handicap). Some of these situations are common enough to permit us to generalize about them.

But before deciding that a private school is the only solution for your child, you might consider some alternatives. To begin with, almost all communities change—often rapidly—and your own move may be representative of the change. If, for example, you have had to move into a low-income rural area because your employer has decided to set up a research facility where land is cheap and taxes are low, you may be certain that many of your coworkers will be equally dissatisfied with the local system and will join forces with you to improve it.

Many schools in central North Carolina, for example, improved dramatically and quickly after the establishment of Research Triangle Park attracted a population of scientists, engineers, and other professionals who

PER PUPIL EXPENDITURES ON EDUCATION BY STATES, 1992

UNITED STATES	5,466	Missouri	4,534
Alabama	3,675	Montana	5,127
Alaska	9,248	Nebraska	4,676
Arizona	4,750	Nevada	4,910
Arkansas	3,770	New Hampshire	5,500
California	4,686	New Jersey	10,219
Colorado	5,259	New Mexico	4,692
Connecticut	8,299	New York	8,658
Delaware	6,080	North Carolina	4,857
Dist. of Col.	8,116	North Dakota	4,119
Florida	5,639	Ohio	5,451
Georgia	4,720	Oklahoma	3,939
Hawaii	5,453	Oregon	5,972
Idaho	3,528	Pennsylvania	6,980
Illinois	5,248	Rhode Island	6,834
Indiana	5,429	South Carolina	4,537
Iowa	4,949	South Dakota	4,255
Kansas	5,131	Tennessee	3,736
Kentucky	4,616	Texas	4,651
Louisiana	4,378	Utah	3,092
Maine	5,969	Vermont	6,992
Maryland	6,273	Virginia	5,487
Massachusetts	6,323	Washington	5,331
Michigan	5,630	West Virginia	5,415
Minnesota	5,510	Wisconsin	5,972
Mississippi	3,344	Wyoming	5,333

insisted that the local school system prepare their children adequately for college. Some school systems in southern New Hampshire showed similar rapid improvement with the influx of large numbers of professionals who worked in Massachusetts but who preferred to live across the state line in neighboring New Hampshire.

Of course, this argument may strike you as rather abstract and remote, but it may also prompt you to ask yourself (and perhaps your neighbors) what you might accomplish if you were to keep your child in a public school and work toward improving it instead of making a convenient, if expensive, escape from the public system.

A more immediate solution to the problem of inadequate local schools is to investigate the possibility of enrolling your child in a public school in a neighboring community. In general, the public school system of a town in which a university is located is superior to those of the surrounding communities—because university faculty members are understandably concerned with the quality of the education their children receive and are willing to pay taxes to support it. For the same reason, affluent suburbs usually have better school systems than the poorer rural towns that may border them. Not all such school systems accept "outsiders," and those that do are likely to charge an annual fee of $1,000 to $4,000 for students whose parents are not local taxpayers, but such an arrangement is not uncommon and, even though it involves making arrangements for transportation, it is likely to be far less costly than a private school.

Yet another alternative is to make up for the inadequacies of the local school by supplementing it with your own efforts. Instead of merely helping your child with homework, you can use the homework as a springboard for further and more complex learning. If you stimulate an early interest in reading, the child is likely to explore the local library endlessly on his own. And if you spend vacations doing interesting things in interesting places instead of visiting the passive and prefabricated pleasures of Disneyland or Epcot, the child is likely to develop new interests and extend existing ones. Of course, this involves your own time and energy, and sending the child off to a private school can save both. But it can be rather costly in terms of satisfaction as well as money.

A "Difficult" Child   Although the "problems" of many children consist only of their failure to meet their parents' unrealistic expectations, there is no doubt that some children suffer from very real physical, emotional, or mental handicaps—and that these may be aggravated by insensitive teachers or inappropriate placement in class. Unfortunately, sending the child off to a private school, although it moves the problem out of the parents' immediate environment, may not solve it.

The first step toward a solution is correct diagnosis, and this is often difficult. Failure to learn to read, for example, is frequently diagnosed as mental retardation or as an emotional problem when, in fact, it may be due to poor eyesight or to dyslexia—that is, difficulties in perception which have nothing to do with mental retardation and which apparently become much less of a handicap as the child grows older. It is easy to see the damage that can be inflicted on both the child and the parents when dyslexia is misdiagnosed. Similarly, behavioral difficulties are often assumed to be the child's problem when, in fact, they are caused or aggravated by parents or siblings. So, too, children have been diagnosed as hyperactive when, in fact, their inappropriately high level of activity was caused by their excruciating boredom in a class taught at a level far below their potential. If you accept such diagnoses without seeking a second opinion, you may be doomed to years of very expensive frustration.

Proper diagnosis can be time-consuming, expensive, and exasperating—especially if you live in a community with few resources for medical and psychological consultation. But the additional cost involved in getting an objective evaluation from a distant clinic or hospital—especially one connected with a university medical school—is a good investment if it prevents you from believing the false promises offered by a private school that has an obvious financial interest in enrolling your child.

It's Not Forever

Fortunately, a wrong decision about private vs. public schooling is not fatal. If you try a private school and it turns out to be a disappointment, you will have lost a year's fee but you won't have damaged your child. Children are remarkably resilient and, although most of them become temporarily unhappy at the prospect of changing schools and making new friends, this kind of change is extremely common, and it usually enriches the child's experience without doing him any lasting harm. It is only if you switch from one school to another every year because none of them seem to solve the problem that you should become concerned. Perhaps you are asking the school to do something that no school can do and that requires a careful examination of what is going on with the child when she or he is not in class.

C H A P T E R 5

THE TEEN YEARS

There's a widespread belief that when children enter their teens the family home becomes a battleground and that fullscale fights or intermittent skirmishes continue until the child leaves for college, marriage, or a separate apartment. But a good deal of solid research indicates that this stereotype has little validity. In most families, the studies conclude, the teenaged children love and respect their parents, adopt essentially the same values as their parents, and live with them in reasonable harmony.

This is not to say that conflicts don't arise. Although they may center on the child's choice of friends, her use of leisure time, or his plans (or lack of plans) for college or a career, they very often involve issues that relate directly to money: allowances and how they should be used, after-school jobs, ownership of a car or some other "set of wheels," and the spending of money on items that are far more attractive to the child than to the parents. But these conflicts, even if they generate a good deal of sound and fury, are usually short-lived, and they're unlikely to produce any long-term alienation between parent and child.

The conflicts arise because, in the process of becoming independent, teenagers need to rebel against their parents, because parents are reluctant or afraid to relinquish full control, and because money is—in both symbolic and real terms—a means of exercising control. But no matter how violent the confrontation, in the long run the child's behavior is likely to be modeled on that of the parents. Parents who are prudent about money find that their children, despite occasional rebellion, are equally prudent. And impulsive, spendthrift parents are likely to produce impulsive, spendthrift children, no matter how earnestly they preach the virtues of caution and thrift.

What may aggravate the parent-child conflict at your house is your growing anxiety over long-term money problems because, as children enter their teen years, the financial burden on their parents inevitably becomes heavier. Medical costs may be lower—because the usual childhood illnesses are past history and the teen years are the healthiest in the life cycle—but orthodontia may take a big bite out of the family budget, especially since it's not usually covered fully by dental insurance. And anyone familiar with the normal teenager's appetite and need for privacy will realize that the costs of food and housing can escalate considerably.

Then, of course, there are the out-of-pocket costs of increasingly expensive clothing, accessories, and recreation. Although some of these items may be bought with earnings from an after-school job, a significant residue is likely to be left for you to pay for, either directly or through an allowance. In addition, there is the question of an automobile and its insurance.

All of these disbursements are more or less to be expected. But there may also be unforeseen expenses: medical or dental bills for an automobile or motorcycle or athletic injury, or legal fees resulting from some teenage prank, or bills for psychological counseling if the emotional problems of adolescence become serious or persistent. Finally, and inevitably, there is the major problem of financing four years of college. These and other expenses will be dealt with in this chapter and the one that follows.

AGE AT WHICH A PERSON[1] CAN LEGALLY:

STATE	Age of majority	Marry w/o parental consent[2]	Marry w/parental consent	Vote	Buy alcohol	Drive
Alabama	19	18	14	18	21	14
Alaska	18	18	16	18	21	14
Arizona	18	18	16	18	21	16
Arkansas	18	18	17M, 16F	18	21	14
California	18	18	5	18	21	16
Colorado	18	18	16	18	21	16
Connecticut	18	18	16	18	21	16
Delaware	18	18	18M, 16F	18	21	16

Perhaps the problems of the teenage period can best be put into perspective by the realization that adulthood is imminent and that, depending on your place of residence, certain forms of behavior are permitted either earlier or later than the age of majority. The table that follows can be viewed, in a sense, as a timetable for possible difficulties or sources of friction.

THE USUAL EXPENSES

The Allowance Question

Even if your child has an after-school job or indulgent and generous grandparents, the bulk of his or her out-of-pocket expenditures is likely to come from the weekly allowance, and the size of this may well become an ongoing issue between you. The actual number of dollars you hand over to your child may, of course, be limited by your income ("Stop nagging! We simply can't afford more" is a perfectly legitimate response to a demand for an increase), but far more important in negotiating the amount is a clear understanding of the underlying purpose of the allowance: to give the child first-hand experience with the saving, spending—and even wasting—of money.

The affluent parent who—in an effort to enhance his image with his daughter and her peers—hands her $100 a week defeats this purpose

Sign a Contract	Write a Will	Work w/Permit	Work w/o Permit[3]	Consent to Medical Care[6]	Leave School	Serve on a Jury
19	19	14	16	19	16	19
18	18	14	17	18	16	18
18	18	NSP	16	18	16	18
18	18	14	16	18	18	18
18	18	14	16	18	16	18
18	18	14	16	18	16	18
18	18	14	16	18	16	18
18	18	14	16	18	16	18

AGE AT WHICH A PERSON[1] CAN LEGALLY:

STATE	Age of majority	Marry w/o parental consent[2]	Marry w/parental consent	Vote	Buy alcohol	Drive
Dist. of Col.	18	18	16	18	21	16
Florida	18	18	16	18	21	15
Georgia	18	16	No age limit	18	21	16
Hawaii	18	18	16	18	21	15
Idaho	18	18	16	18	21	14
Illinois	18	18	16	18	21	16
Indiana	18	18	17	18	21	16
Iowa	18	18	18	18	21	16
Kansas	18	18	Under 16	18	21	14
Kentucky	18	18	5	18	21	16
Louisiana	18	18	18M, 16F	18	21	15
Maine	18	18	16	18	21	16
Maryland	18	18	16	18	21	16
Massachusetts	18	18	5	18	21	16 $^1/_2$
Michigan	18	18	16	18	21	16
Minnesota	18	18	16	18	21	16
Mississippi	18	17M, 15F	Under 17/15	18	21	15
Missouri	18	15	15	18	21	15
Montana	18	16	16	18	21	15
Nebraska	19	17	17	18	21	16
Nevada	18	18	16	18	21	16
New Hampshire	18	18	14M, 13F	18	21	16
New Jersey	18	18	16	18	21	17
New Mexico	18	18	16	18	21	15
New York	18	18	14	18	21	16
North Carolina	18	18	16	18	21	18
North Dakota	18	18	16	18	21	14
Ohio	18	18	18M, 16F	18	21	18
Oklahoma	18	16	16	18	21	15 $^1/_2$
Oregon	18	18	17	18	21	16
Pennsylvania	21	18	16	18	21	16

Sign a Contract	Write a Will	Work w/Permit	Work w/o Permit[3]	Consent to Medical Care[6]	Leave School	Serve on a Jury
18	18	16	18	18	17	18
18	18	16	18	18	16	18
18	18	12	18	18	16	18
18	18	Under 14	18	18	18	18
18	18	NSP	14	18	16	18
18	18	14	16	18	16	18
18	18	14	18	18	16	18
18	18	14	16	18	16	18
18	18	14	16	18	16	18
18	18	14	18	18	16	18
18	18	16	18	18	17	18
18	18	14	16	18	17	18
18	18	14	18	18	16	18
18	18	14	16	18	16	18
18	18	14	18	18	16	18
18	18	14	16	18	16	18
18	18	NSP	14	18	14	21
18	18	14	16	18	16	21
18	18	16	18	18	16	18
19	18	14	16	18	16	19
18	18	14	16	18	17	18
18	18	12	16	18	16	18
18	18	16	18	18	16	18
18	18	14	16	18	18	18
18	18	16	18	18	16	18
18	18	16	18	18	16	18
18	18	14	16	18	16	18
18	18	16	18	18	18	18
18	18	14	16	18	18	18
18	18	14	18	18	18	18
21	18	16	18	18	17	18

AGE AT WHICH A PERSON[1] CAN LEGALLY:

STATE	Age of majority	Marry w/o parental consent[2]	Marry w/parental consent	Vote	Buy alcohol	Drive
Rhode Island	18	18	18M, 16F	18	21	16
South Carolina	18	18	16M, 14F	18	21	15
South Dakota	18	18	16	18	21	14
Tennessee	18	18	16	18	21	16
Texas	18	18	14	18	21	16
Utah	18	18	14	18	21	16
Vermont	18	18	16M, 14F[4]	18	21	16
Virginia	18	18	16	18	21	16
Washington	18	18	17	18	21	16
West Virginia	18	18	18	18	21	16
Wisconsin	18	18	16	18	21	16
Wyoming	19	19	16	18	21	16

NOTES:
M = Male F = Female NSP = No statutory provision
1. Regardless of age, a person may be considered an adult once he/she marries, and consequently may be able to enter into a contract, remarry without parental consent, and perform other acts which would otherwise be prohibited. Service in the armed forces and court-approved emancipation can also confer adult status.
2. Many states waive the minimum age if the female is pregnant or has given birth out of wedlock.

because, assuming that "there's more where that came from," she is likely to become a spendthrift. On the other hand, limiting the allowance to bare necessities deprives the child of experience with "guns-or-butter" decisions and prevents her from learning that money spent on mascara is no longer available for bus fares and ice-cream sundaes.

Perhaps the optimal plan is to agree that the allowance will cover as many expenses as possible—clothing, recreational equipment such as stereos and tennis racquets, and bus fares and field trips as well as the usual school lunches, movie admissions, and the occasional hamburger— and to adjust the allowance accordingly. There is, of course, some risk to this: the child may forgo school lunches in order to buy cassettes or CDs of music that you find intolerable. But you can monitor the child for malnutrition. As for the "waste of money" on the tape cassette, bear in mind that another important purpose of the allowance is to give your child

Sign a Contract	Write a Will	Work w/Permit	Work w/o Permit[3]	Consent to Medical Care[6]	Leave School	Serve on a Jury
18	18	14	16	18	16	18
18	18	NSP	16	18	17	18
18	18	14	16	18	16	18
18	18	14	18	18	17	18
18	18	14	18	18	17	18
18	18	16	16	18	18	18
18	18	14	16	18	16	18
18	18	14	16	18	18	18
18	18	14	18	18	18	18
18	18	14	16	18	16	18
18	18	14	18	18	18	18
19	19	Under 16	16	18	16	18

3. In most states, age restrictions do not apply to domestic work or farm labor.
4. With court permission.
5. No statutory minimum age. Both court permission and parental consent are required.
6. Some states permit a minor to consent to medical care for pregnancy or its termination, substance abuse, psychological disturbance, and diseases that are sexually transmitted or communicable.

some autonomy in *discretionary* spending, and the solution here may be to grit your teeth, buy a set of ear plugs, and hope that your child's taste and judgment will improve.

Unless the allowance agreement is adhered to consistently—that is, if you compassionately "bail out" the child whenever she exhausts her allowance—she is unlikely to learn that money must be spent thoughtfully rather than impulsively or that perhaps some of it should be husbanded for some large purchase several months in the future. Of course, if something occurs that requires an immediate expenditure—the purchase of a mountain bike at a one-day, half-price sale, for example—there is no reason why you can't advance the money and recoup it through "payroll deductions." But this doesn't imply an attitude of impersonal rigidity. Not only do birthdays and other special events call for a generous and impulsive gift, but such gifts can be given spontaneously, when the child wants something—a new flute, for example, or ballet lessons—that her allowance can't possibly cover.

Should the child's allowance be a quid pro quo for services rendered—for taking out the garbage regularly or mowing the lawn, for example, or clearing the dinner table nightly? Most child-rearing experts think not. Children, they argue, should be taught that, as family members, they have certain responsibilities and that they should fulfill these without payment. On the other hand, if you are in a situation that requires paid help—for typing your correspondence in a small business, for example, or for clerking in a family-operated store—there is no reason why you should not hire your own child rather than a stranger.

An After-School Job

Although the issue of a job after school often creates conflict between parent and child, neither parents nor children take a consistently pro or con position. Some parents virtually insist that the child work after school; others argue strongly against it. Some children are very eager to work; others reject the minimum-wage jobs that are available and prefer to "hang out" and subsist on their allowances. It may be useful, therefore, to review both sides of the arguments that are most commonly employed by either side.

"It Will Teach Him (Her) that Money Doesn't Grow on Trees." There's little doubt that looking for a job can give a teenager first-hand experience with the difficulties an unskilled person faces in finding employment—experience that may stimulate not only sympathy with the unskilled unemployed but also a recognition of the economic value of more education. There is even less doubt that frying hamburgers for hours on end at the minimum wage will make vivid the fact that "this pair of designer sunglasses will cost me six hours of work at the griddle at McDonald's." But whether these useful lessons require long-term commitment to a regular after-school job is another matter. Often they can be learned through a short (and possibly unsuccessful) stint of job-hunting or an occasional job of snow-shoveling or lawn-mowing or baby-sitting. And too often they are not learned at all. The youngster who argues that an after-school job "beats sitting around doing nothing" may take an easy-come, easy-go attitude toward his earnings and fritter them away on frivolities.

"It Will Teach Him (Her) Something about Business." At the turn of the century an after-school job—helping out the local druggist or butcher or cabinetmaker—not only taught a youngster how a business was run but often served as an entry to a career. But today these apprenticeship jobs have all but vanished. Bagging groceries at a supermarket will teach

a youngster no more about the complexities of supermarket operation than cooking french fries will teach her about running a fast-food franchise. Pumping gas at one of the few remaining full-service stations won't teach him about automotive repairs because the trained mechanic will have no time to spend teaching him, nor will he have time to learn. Will running a newspaper route teach him the fundamentals of capitalism? It may teach him to get up on time and to keep his accounts accurately, but these habits can be learned as easily in an early-morning math class—where his parent doesn't have to fill in for him when he's in bed with a fever.

There are a few—very few—jobs that are worth having because they can offer the youngster a glimpse of a career in which he has some interest: volunteer work in a hospital or a social agency, for example, or helping out at a veterinary clinic or a day-care center, or working as a mail person or messenger in the office of a magazine or newspaper. These jobs pay little or nothing, and they're not easy to find, but they may have far more long-term value than the more available routine service jobs to which most youngsters gravitate.

"I Need the Money!" Since some teenagers' "need" for money is insatiable, the validity of the "I need the money" argument depends on what the child's allowance is intended to cover and what "extras" the parents provide for out of their own pockets. If the child needs the money to pay for an expensive and long-lasting item—a sophisticated camera, for example, or a computer or a ten-speed bike—working for it may actually increase his appreciation of it, even if the parents agree to match his earnings on a dollar-for-dollar basis. Similarly, although no after-school job is likely to provide enough money for a college education, it can make up some of the difference between a less-expensive and more-expensive college, or it can meet some of the many college expenses beyond basic tuition, room, board, and books.

On the other hand, some teenagers who are very eager to own a car will find a job at some distance from home and then insist that they need a car to get to and from work, promising to pay for the car with their earnings. Car ownership is an issue that needs to be decided on its own merits (see pp. 106–111), but the child needs to recognize (and to know that you recognize) what comes first in this chicken-or-the-egg situation.

Similarly, if the child "needs" the money only to keep up with the teenaged Joneses in terms of fad clothing, cosmetics, CDs, and similar items, he may well find himself spending valuable hours working to increase the profits of manufacturers and retailers. Here the parent needs to consider whether an admittedly valuable lesson—the child's ultimate realization that he has wasted his money—is worth the waste of his time.

"It Won't Interfere with School." Whether an after-school job will affect the child's school work depends on the number of hours worked weekly, the shift worked, and the child's attitude toward school. Studies indicate that although working twenty hours weekly or less does not affect school performance, a longer work week does. But one issue is whether the twenty hours are subtracted from rather unproductive leisure time or from homework and from interesting and valuable after-school activities.

More important, although the studies show that teenagers who work more than twenty hours a week tend to have lower school grades, they don't make clear that the work *causes* the poor grades. Many children who receive poor grades are attracted to work because it provides them with a level of self-esteem that they can't achieve in the classroom. If you suspect that this is true of your own child, you might try to persuade him that a job bagging groceries at the supermarket is not a long-range solution to his problem.

Because the "work ethic" is so highly valued in our society, we tend to give an extra helping of respect and admiration to successful people who "worked their way through college." But, although the soaring cost of college forces many undergraduates to work, although many college scholarships are tied to a work program, and although some students have made very sound career choices on the basis of their campus job experience, the fact remains that college students who work generally don't achieve grades as high as those who don't work.

In general, then, the to-work-or-not-to-work question depends on a number of circumstances. One thing is clear: the number of interesting and educational part-time jobs is falling just as rapidly as the number of dull, dead-end, minimum-wage "service" jobs is rising. As a result, most after-school jobs involve nothing more than an exchange of the child's time and unskilled labor for a certain number of dollars. If the child's need for money is genuine and if the earnings will be used productively, then a job can be a valuable experience in earning, saving, and spending money. But involvement in productive leisure activities also has value, although this is often overlooked in a society that places a high premium on work for its own sake.

A SET OF WHEELS

If you've been disappointed at having produced no sons, the issue of car ownership should bring you vast compensatory comfort. Teenaged daughters are far less likely than sons to demand a car of their own and—because they do their driving in less hazardous situations—the cost of their insurance premiums, uninsured fender-benders, and traffic fines is likely to be lower than it is for male children. You may, of course, worry about the behavior of the dates with whom they go driving, but that is not a financial problem.

Quite aside from its practical uses, a car has such high symbolic value in our society that, unless you live in Manhattan or some other congested metropolis, your son is likely to begin agitating for a car of his own (or, at least, unrestricted access to the family car) some months before he reaches the age of licensing in your state. If, like any normal parent, you are hesitant about this, you will be able to deal with the issue more effectively if you recognize that it's not a simple one—that it has social-psychological and safety aspects as well as financial.

The Social-Psychological Aspects

In American society, the acquisition of a driver's license is what anthropologists call a "rite of passage," because it marks an important and conspicuous step toward adulthood. A good deal of parental resistance, then, stems simply from a reluctance to see "our little boy" grow up. But there are realistic considerations, too. The fact is that a car offers the child both mobility and privacy—the opportunity to drive to places where he can't be identified and a private space in which to be alone with his peers and to experiment with sex, alcohol, and other drugs. Small wonder, then, that parents worry.

But a moment's sober reflection will lead you to conclude that adolescents *do* need privacy for all kinds of experimentation (think back to your own teen years) and, although one traffic expert suggested that giving each adolescent access to a private apartment for these activities would reduce the highway crash rate, his proposal has not yet been adopted. And the fact is that if you try to stop the normal process of maturation, you will be no more successful than King Canute.

It is possible, too, that your child needs a car simply in order to have a normal social life. Very few parts of the country have adequate systems of mass transit, and many suburbs have been laid out so as to make a car essential for shopping, visiting, going to the dentist or a music lesson, and all the other normal out-of-the-house activities. Any parent who has spent a number of years as the children's chauffeur may regard the child's licensing as a very welcome release from bondage.

The Question of Safety

There is, of course, no question that the highway is a dangerous place, especially for teenagers. But two important facts may offer you some reassurance. First, although it is true that both the accident and the fatality rates are much higher for young males than for any other group, such accidents, despite the publicity they get, are infrequent events. The overwhelming majority of teenagers do *not* get killed or injured, although minor fender-benders caused by inexperience are shockingly expensive and not uncommon.

Second—and perhaps more important—a study of the driving records of 8,000 young males found that the best predictor of their driving behavior was *the father's driving behavior for the three years prior to the son's licensure.* In simpler terms, the fathers whose records were free of violations and crashes had sons whose records were equally clean. The fathers with numerous violations and crashes had sons whose records resembled theirs. This doesn't mean, of course, that driving skill is genetically transmitted. It means that, on the road, as in other contexts, sons imitate their fathers' behavior. These findings may reassure you, but if they cause you to worry, you may still have time to change your own driving behavior.

On the other hand, these like-father-like-son findings, because they are statistical, mask the fact that there are exceptions. The emphasis on teenaged drunk drivers tends to obscure the fact that some nice, well-behaved sons of cautious, conventional fathers get into serious and costly accidents not as a result of alcohol but simply because they are inexperienced. In addition, studies show that most police officers are prejudiced against teenaged drivers and hence prone to designate them as culpable on their accident report. And since your son, through simple inexperience, *may* have a front-end collision that will cost his date most of her front teeth and permanent disfigurement, it's a good idea to make sure that he has sufficient medical and liability insurance coverage.

Economic Options

If your child's need for access to a car is genuine—or if his desire for it is irresistible—you have several options, each with very different costs. If you want to indulge in conspicuous consumption—or one-up your friends and neighbors—you can buy him a brand-new car as a graduation gift. (High-priced sports cars seem to be favored by this kind of parent.) But bear in mind that the value of a new car depreciates 30% the first year, provided that your child manages to keep its body work intact, and that collision coverage on a new car is expensive. The same money conservatively invested in stocks, bonds, or other investment instruments will appreciate for as long as the child holds on to it. And the same money spent on a trip to Europe may produce skills and memories that will last the child's entire lifetime. In addition, a car of his own may tempt the child to spend more time in it than his actual needs justify.

A much more economic option—at least for the first year or two—involves giving the child the use of one or more of the family cars with strict specification of the times when and the purposes for which he may use it and a clear understanding that all driving privileges will be canceled if the conditions are violated. This option not only eliminates the investment and depreciation costs on a separate vehicle but is likely to reduce insurance premiums, since it costs less to add the child as an "additional driver" responsible for only a small percentage of your car's annual mileage than to pay a premium for him as owner or driver of a new vehicle. Requiring him to pay the additional insurance premium as well as his share of the gasoline and maintenance expenses can make him realize vividly the actual per-mile costs of driving.

If sharing one of the family cars is not practical, it may make sense to buy a three- or four-year-old used car that has been carefully checked by a mechanic of your choice. Whether to register this car in your name or his depends on a number of factors—on whether, for example, you will be entitled to a multiple-vehicle insurance discount if you assume ownership, on the amount of your liability insurance coverage, on whether cars are taxed as personal property in your state, and on whether your ownership of the car can restrict the child's excessive use of it. The table below indicates relative costs of these options.

INSURING A MALE DRIVER AGE 16–18[*]

The annual premiums shown here (for illustrative purposes only) assume liability coverage of $100,000 per person and $300,000 per accident as well as collision coverage ($250 deductible) on a vehicle worth $5,000 without medical coverage. For medical coverage, add $220 to each annual premium.

Son uses family-owned car and is listed as "occasional" driver (Multiple vehicle discount in force)	$ 800.00
Son uses family-owned car and is listed as "primary" driver (Multiple vehicle discount in force)	$1,414.00
Son uses car owned by himself	$1,714.00

[*]Rates provided by AAA of Michigan, as of June, 1994.

Although the alternative listed first in the table seems to be the obvious choice, bear in mind that your ownership of the vehicle exposes you to liability if your son becomes culpably involved in a serious accident and the judgment against him exceeds your insurance coverage. If, on the other hand, he is the sole owner, only he is legally responsible and, if he has few or no assets of his own, any judgment against him in excess of existing liability insurance coverage will be uncollectible.

There are a couple of further alternatives—both of them probably undesirable. The first—very popular with male teenagers who fancy themselves as good mechanics—is to let the child buy and rehabilitate a "junker." Because few teenagers are as mechanically adept as they think they are, because auto repair often requires expensive, specialized tools, and because "bargain" cars are very rarely bargains, this is not a good arrangement unless (1) you yourself are an expert and well-equipped mechanic with time to spare, or (2) you are cheerful about getting out of bed at 2. A.M. on a Sunday morning to rescue your child who is marooned at a party ten miles from home because his own vehicle won't start.

Another alternative—which may be proposed by the child either with great enthusiasm or as a money-saving compromise—is the purchase of a motorcycle. On economic grounds this provides little advantage if any, because in recent years the cost of a new motorcycle has approached the cost of a compact car, insurance coverage is disproportionately expensive, and fuel economy has been dropping steadily. And used motorcycles are even less reliable than used cars.

In addition, motorcycles are many times more hazardous than cars— regardless of how careful the driver may be. More than half of all motorcycle fatalities turn out to be the fault of a motorist, not the cyclist, and your child's earnest promise that he will "drive carefully" offers neither you nor him any reassurance. Moreover, in motorcycle crashes, the pillion passenger is at least as likely to be killed as the driver, and the prospect of your financial and emotional liability if this should happen while your son is out on a date with a friend riding behind does not bear thinking about.

A close relative of the motorcycle as a form of minimal transportation is the motor scooter. This is especially attractive to youngsters who are under the age of licensure, because in some states neither the driver nor the vehicle needs to be licensed or insured. These vehicles embody all the hazards of a motorcycle and a couple of extra ones: they are too under-powered for safe use on a highway and they are far less stable than a motorcycle. Both these factors should persuade you to respond with a firm "No" to any suggestions about a motor scooter.

Decisions, Decisions

Because arguments about the use or purchase of a car can grow rather intense, it's important to realize that the issue is short-lived, extending only from the minimum age of licensure (16 in most states) to the age of majority (18 in most states). Once the child becomes an adult, you have no legal or financial responsibility for—and no control over—his ownership or use of a car titled solely in his name. Perhaps the best approach—for your sake and his—is to teach him, by example as well as by precept, that a car is an expensive but useful tool rather than a symbol of adulthood or a means of showing off or venting the inevitable frustrations of life.

MISCHANCE AND MISBEHAVIOR

Before the child's teen years, you were either legally or morally responsible for any damages the child caused—to himself or to others—but this liability was likely to be limited to a medical bill for the treatment of a broken arm or leg or to the replacement of an occasional window-pane broken by a wildly thrown baseball. The teen years, however, bring with them an increase in both the number of risks and their potential costs. For example, the exposure to serious athletic injury, either as a player or as a spectator, can have costly consequences, as can such normal teen activities as riding around in the cars of friends and such common misbehaviors as vandalism and shoplifting.

Athletic Injuries

Although athletic injuries that require medical attention—and that can result in long-term disability—are far more common than is generally believed, there is little information on their costs. In many such situations the medical costs may be covered by the parents' health insurance coverage, but relatively few such policies cover dental work—an all too common outcome of a mishap on the football, soccer, or lacrosse field or the basketball court. The question arises, then, as to whether parents can successfully bring suit against the school to recover medical or dental costs and to compensate the victim for pain and suffering.

In general, few parents file suit against the school system in such situations—partly owing to ignorance of their rights, partly out of reluctance to cause problems for the coach or the school, and partly because the courts generally hold that anyone participating in a sport that can produce injury is aware of, and hence assumes, the risks involved.

But there are several circumstances in which the courts have held the school system liable. If, for example, the coach knew that a player was temporarily unfit physically or was wearing inadequate equipment and nevertheless sent him into a practice session, the coach (and hence the school system) can be held responsible. The same holds true if the school fails to provide prompt and competent medical care immediately following an injury or if a referee in a wrestling match fails to break up a hold that can produce injury. In short, negligence on the part of the school system can render it liable for damages.

Injuries to spectators at school games are also common when, for example, a ball goes out of bounds, but here again the courts have generally held that spectators, like players, assume the risks inherent in the event. But here, too, the school can be held liable if it is found to be negligent—if, for example, it failed to provide spectator protection at a hockey game or if a construction defect or lack of maintenance causes the bleachers to collapse.

The fact that your health insurance coverage pays for the treatment of your child's injuries should not deter you from bringing suit against the school if your claim has merit. For one thing, the cost of such treatment inevitably raises insurance premiums. For another, your health plan may pay only for direct medical treatment and not for the considerable incidental expenses that result from the hospitalization or long-term home care of a child. And, lastly, a substantial damage award may persuade schools to exercise a good deal more care in their supervision of athletes.

Vehicular Injuries

There are several situations in which your child may be involved in an injury-producing automobile or motorcycle accident. She may get hurt while driving her car. She may escape injury herself but injure one or more passengers. She may be injured as a passenger in someone else's car. And in the first two of these situations, she may or may not be found to be culpable in causing the accident. The question of your personal liability in each of these situations depends on two facts: the ownership of the vehicle and the existence of no-fault insurance in your state. The various possible consequences are shown in the table on page 114.

Emotional Problems

Adolescence is the time at which a number of mental and emotional problems make their appearance—ranging from devastating but rare schizophrenia to mild but rather common maladjustments that can make for troubled relationships with peers or with parents, teachers, the police, and other authorities. As the extent of this phenomenon has become recognized, sources of help—individual psychiatrists and psychologists, social agencies, and counseling centers—have become increasingly available, not only in metropolitan areas but also in suburbs and small towns.

But many parents fail to use these resources. Some are convinced that the child is simply "going through a stage" that will disappear with the passage of time. Others feel that seeking professional help is a clear admission of their incompetence as parents or that they will be found at fault if they are invited to participate in the therapeutic process. Still others acknowledge that professional help might be effective but feel that they simply can't afford the cost of what may be a long period of therapy, especially since very few health-insurance policies cover the costs of emotional illnesses.

There is little we can do to change the minds of the resistant parents, but to those who see money as the major obstacle we can suggest that they may have in mind a form of therapy that has been pretty much outmoded: the five-times-a-week Freudian psychoanalysis at $200 a session that can drag on for several years. Three relatively recent developments have produced a wide number of alternatives to this stereotype.

First, a number of new styles and techniques of therapy and counseling have been developed which are much briefer (and hence much less expensive) than traditional Freudian psychoanalysis. Group therapy, for example, allows several individuals who share a behavior problem to share the costs of a single therapist. And family therapy, in which several or all members of the family are involved in the process, often produces more effective results much more quickly than individual therapy. Even the course of individual therapy has been shortened by therapists who take a more directive approach than the traditional free-association-on-the-couch analysts.

Second, because so many people have been attracted to clinical psychology as a profession, there is now, in many communities, sufficient competition among them to have lowered the hourly cost of private treatment. These newcomers are likely to be young (an advantage when dealing with adolescents) and well trained in modern techniques.

LIABILITY FOR CHILD INVOLVED IN A
MOTOR-VEHICLE ACCIDENT

Situation	In "Fault" State	In "No-fault" State	
		Economic Damages[1]	Noneconomic Damages[2]
Child driving own car, injured by own negligence	Child	Child's insurer	Child
Child driving own car, injured by other's negligence	Driver, owner, and insurer of other vehicle	Child's insurer	Driver, owner, and insurer of other vehicle
Child driving own car, passenger injured by child's negligence[3]	Child and his insurer	Passenger's insurer[4]	Child and his insurer
Child driving own car, passenger injured by other's negligence	Driver, owner, and insurer of other vehicle	Passenger's insurer[4]	Driver, owner, and insurer of other vehicle
Child driving own car, pedestrian injured by child's negligence	Child and his insurer	Pedestrian's insurer[4]	Child and his insurer
Child driving own car, negligently injures occupant of another car	Child and his insurer	Occupant's insurer[4]	Child and his insurer
Child driving parent's car, injured by own negligence[5]	Child	Parent's insurer	Child
Child driving parent's car, injured by another's negligence	Driver, owner, and insurer of other vehicle	Parent's insurer	Driver, owner, and insurer of other vehicle
Child driving parent's car, passenger injured through child's negligence[3]	Child, parent, and parent's insurer	Passenger's insurer[4]	Child, parent, and parent's insurer
Child driving parent's car, passenger injured through another's negligence	Driver, owner, and insurer of other vehicle	Passenger's insurer[4]	Driver, owner, and insurer of other vehicle
Child driving parent's car, pedestrian injured through child's negligence	Child, parent, and parent's insurer	Pedestrian's insurer[4]	Child, parent, and parent's insurer

Situation	In "Fault" State	In "No-fault" State	
		Economic Damages	Noneconomic Damages
Child driving parent's car, negligently injures occupant of another car	Child, parent, and parent's insurer	Occupant's insurer[4]	Child, parent, and parent's insurer

NOTES:
1. Economic damages include hospital and medical bills and wage losses.
2. Noneconomic damages include pain, suffering, scarring, and disfigurement.
3. In some states "guest passenger" laws require a nonpaying passenger seeking damages from his host driver or the driver's insurer to prove that his driver was guilty of gross rather than simple negligence.
4. If the injured person has no no-fault insurance of his own, some states require him to look to the no-fault insurer of other members of his household. If there is none, he may recover his economic damages from the child's no-fault insurer.
5. Most states recognize the "family doctrine," which holds the owner of a vehicle liable for any accidents caused by the negligent driving of his family members if he has consented to their driving the vehicle. Express consent is not always required. Implied consent may be assumed if it is usual for a spouse or a child to drive the family vehicle.

Lastly, many social agencies and other nonprofit organizations, recognizing the burden that private treatment places on middle-income parents, offer therapeutic services on a sliding scale of fees, the cost being adjustable to family income. There is no reason to feel that you are a "welfare case" if you apply to such an organization. You may, in fact, be the very client for which such services have been established.

The question of whether you are getting good value for the money you spend on your child's therapy is, unfortunately, almost impossible to answer. Studies comparing the effectiveness of various types of therapy seem to conclude that the method used has less influence on success than the quality of the relationship between the therapist and the patient. But this is a rather shaky criterion because, all too often, patients in the early stages dislike the therapist intensely simply because the therapist is forcing the patient to examine his or her behavior in ways that make him intensely uncomfortable. Choosing the right therapist is inevitably chancy, but if your state has rigorous licensing requirements or if you use a reputable referral service, you are unlikely to go wrong. There are, of course, some incompetents and charlatans in the fields of psychological counseling and therapy but, despite popular opinion to the contrary, they are no more numerous than in other professions.

Vandalism, Shoplifting, and Other Delinquencies

In one plot that is quite common in parents' nightmares, their adolescent child—usually male—gets into serious trouble and the parent wakes in a cold sweat wondering, "Am I going to be held responsible for this?" Whether the "trouble" involves extensive damage to a neighbor's house by a gang of classmates flushed with victory after a school football game or your son's embarrassed disclosure that he has impregnated the 16-year-old next door, the question of parental responsibility is a real one. The answer, however, is not simple.

To begin with, some states have legislation which makes parents financially responsible for any damage caused by their children. But because these laws were passed in order to discourage delinquency by motivating parents to monitor the behavior of their children more closely, the maximum dollar amount of liability in most states does not exceed $2,500.

Moreover, the question of *intent* is significant. If your son, in the course of some friendly roughhousing at a classmate's house accidentally smashes an antique vase, the damage claim (less the deductible) is payable by your

PARENTAL LIABILITY FOR CHILDREN'S TORTS

STATE	Are parents liable?[1]	Age limits	Liability limit for each tort ($)	Kind of tort to which liability extends
Alabama	Yes[2]	Under 18	500	Willful misconduct
Alaska	Yes	Under 18	2,000[3]	Willful misconduct
Arizona	Yes	Under 18	2,500	Willful misconduct
Arkansas	Yes[2]	Under 18	2,000[3]	Willful misconduct
California	Yes	Under 18	10,000	Willful misconduct
Colorado	Yes[2]	Under 18	3,500[3]	Willful misconduct
Connecticut	Yes[2]	Under 18	3,000	Willful misconduct
Delaware	Yes	Under 18	5,000[3]	Willful misconduct
Dist. of Col.	No	Common law applies.[4]		
Florida	Yes[2]	Under 18	2,500[3]	Willful misconduct

1. In all states parental liability terminates when the child marries, enters the armed services, or is emancipated by a court order.
2. No liability unless child is living with parent.

homeowner's policy and your son, not you, remains responsible for the deductible. On the other hand, if your son vandalizes your neighbor's house and grounds, your neighbor can be compensated for the damage (less the deductible) through his homeowner's policy, because it protects him against vandalism. Again, your son, not you, remains responsible for the deductible. Homeowners' policies protect the insured against negligence but not against intentional behavior by members of his own family, but they protect the insured against both kinds of acts by an outsider. If the victim of your child's vandalism is not adequately insured, your child is responsible, although the laws of your state may hold you responsible up to the statutory maximum.

Thus far it would seem that a parent is not inevitably responsible for damage done by his children—not even if he encouraged his son to have heterosexual intercourse with his peers and this behavior resulted in rape or unwanted pregnancy. But this general rule has a couple of exceptions. First, if the parent allows the child unsupervised access to an inherently dangerous object (a gun, for example, or a vehicle that the child was not licensed to operate) and damage ensues, the parent may be held fully responsible. More generally, parents may be held liable if the court

STATE	Are parents liable?[1]	Age limits	Liability limit for each tort ($)	Kind of tort to which liability extends
Georgia	Yes	Under 18	5,000[3]	Willful misconduct
Hawaii	Yes	Under 18	No stated limit	Damage by any tort
Idaho	Yes[2]	Under 18	1,500[3]	Willful misconduct
Illinois	Yes[2]	Under 18	1,000	Willful misconduct
Indiana	Yes[2]	Under 18	2,500[3]	Willful misconduct
Iowa	Yes	Under 18	1,000	Unlawful acts
Kansas	Yes[2]	Under 18	1,000	Willful misconduct
Kentucky	Yes	Under 18	2,500[3]	Willful misconduct
Louisiana	Yes[2]	Under 18	No stated limit	Damage by any tort
Maine	Yes[2]	7–17	800[3]	Willful misconduct
Maryland	Yes[2]	Under 18	5,000	Delinquent acts

3. Parent's liability is limited to property damage and does not extend to personal injury or death.
4. Common law rules typically hold parents liable for neglecting to exercise reasonable supervision of their children.

determines that the parents "failed to control or restrain" the child, knowing that the child might embark on a course of harmful behavior. Lastly, if the child causes damage while acting as a paid employee of a parent—if, for example, the child injures someone with his bicycle on his way to the post office to mail packages for the family business—the parent becomes fully responsible, just as he or she would for the actions of any other employee.

Some Voluntary Expenditures

Thus far we have discussed your legal responsibilities without regard to your parental concerns for your child. If your relationship both with your child and with your neighbors is comfortable, you may very well decide to make good any damages caused by your child without involving an insurance claim. Similarly, you may want to help the child

PARENTAL LIABILITY FOR CHILDREN'S TORTS

STATE	Are parents liable?[1]	Age limits	Liability limit for each tort ($)	Kind of tort to which liability extends
Massachusetts	Yes[2]	7–18	5,000	Willful misconduct
Michigan	Yes[2]	Under 18	2,500	Willful misconduct
Minnesota	Yes[2]	Under 18	500	Willful misconduct
Mississippi	Yes	10–18	2,000[3]	Willful misconduct
Missouri	Yes[2]	Under 18	2,000	Willful misconduct
Montana	Yes[2]	Under 18	1,500[3]	Willful misconduct
Nebraska	Yes	Under 19	1,000	Willful misconduct
Nevada	Yes	Under 18	10,000	Willful misconduct
New Hampshire	No	Common law applies[4]		
New Jersey	Yes	Under 18	No stated limit	Willful misconduct
New Mexico	Yes[2]	Under 18	4,000	Willful misconduct
New York	Yes	10–18	1,000[3]	Willful misconduct
North Carolina	Yes[2]	Under 18	500[3]	Willful misconduct
North Dakota	Common law applies[4]			
Ohio	Yes[2]	Under 18	2,000	Willful misconduct

make restitution for shoplifting even if your state law exempts you from this responsibility.

Perhaps more important, you may find occasion to spend money to protect or support your child's interests even when no damage claim is pending. In a number of U.S. Supreme Court cases involving the civil rights of high school students, the plaintiffs were students who were personally affected by capricious and arbitrary decisions by teachers or administrators. The parents of these students were sufficiently moved by what they saw as abuse of their child to begin suit in the child's behalf. Even though the American Civil Liberties Union eventually came to the aid of some of these parents, a number of them used their own funds to initiate litigation. You may feel, as some of them did, that the cost of this litigation was a small price to pay to demonstrate support for your child and to memorialize it by having his or her name attached to a Supreme Court decision.

STATE	Are parents liable?[1]	Age limits	Liability limit for each tort ($)	Kind of tort to which liability extends
Oklahoma	Yes[2]	Under 18	1,500	Criminal acts
Oregon	Yes[2]	Under 18	5,000	Intentional torts
Pennsylvania	Yes	Under 18	1,000	Willful misconduct
Rhode Island	Yes	Under 18	1,500	Willful misconduct
South Carolina	Yes[2]	Under 18	5,000[3]	Malicious acts
South Dakota	Yes[2]	Under 18	1,500	Willful misconduct
Tennessee	Yes[2]	Under 18	10,000	Willful misconduct
Texas	Yes	12–18	15,000	Willful misconduct
Utah	Yes	Under 18	1,000	Willful misconduct
Vermont	Yes	Under 17	250	Willful misconduct
Virginia	Yes[2]	Under 18	750[3]	Willful misconduct
Washington	Yes[2]	Under 18	3,000	Willful misconduct
West Virginia	Yes[2]	Under 18	2,500[3]	Willful misconduct
Wisconsin	Yes	Under 18	2,500	Willful misconduct
Wyoming	Yes	10–17	2,000[3]	Willful misconduct

CHAPTER 6

THE QUESTION OF COLLEGE

Although "how am I going to pay for my child's college education?" may have been your principal concern ever since your child was born, the question "Which college is the best choice?" becomes even more important as high school graduation approaches. In Chapter 2 we dealt in some detail with the various ways of accumulating a nest egg to pay for your child's college education. But in the long run, making a poor choice can be far more troubling than making the right choice and struggling to pay its costs.

Actually, aside from your home, a four-year college education may well be the largest expenditure you'll ever make. And the chances are that, even if you and your spouse both hold college degrees, you probably know even less about choosing a college than you do about checking out the condition of a house or a used car before you buy it. Before buying the house or the car, you can protect yourself against disappointment by hiring a building inspector or a mechanic to do an inspection—though some people fall in love with a house or a car and buy it despite an expert's strongly negative report.

But evaluating a college is much trickier, because the "condition" of the college is only one factor; far more important is the match between the college and your child's needs and aspirations. What complicates the situation even further is the likelihood that you and your child may have conflicting sets of preferences, preconceptions, and prejudices that have very little to do with reality.

WHAT KIND OF COLLEGE?

Because a mistake in choosing a college can be far more costly than choosing one with very high tuition and board costs, it may be useful, before considering your options in paying for a college education, to examine the validity of some of the preconceptions that are widely held by parents and children and that often govern their choice of college. Don't be surprised if, in the next few pages, you recognize some of your own firm beliefs.

"It's the Ivy League or Nothing!"

The fact that many more cars on the road sport on their rear windows Harvard, Cornell, or Dartmouth decals than decals spelling out Lansing Community College or Southern Illinois University—even though the latter enroll far more undergraduates than the former—is a clear indication that many parents regard a son or daughter attending an Ivy League school as a splendid status symbol and a fine opportunity for school-name-dropping at cocktail parties.

When this kind of parental ego-gratification is a major factor in the decision, it offers both the parent and the child two possibilities for trouble: First, the child, no matter how impressive his academic record, may be rejected, because, although the number of college applicants has fallen in recent years, the Ivy League schools are still cruelly selective, and grades are by no means their only entrance criterion. In this situation, rejection can be very painful, even though it may be due to sheer luck rather than personal deficiency. Second, even if the child is accepted, she may not realize the several advantages attributed to an Ivy League education.

What are these advantages—both real and mythical? To begin with, to judge by the careers of Ivy League graduates, it's apparent that an Ivy League diploma is attractive both to employers and to the admissions committees of professional schools, such as law and medicine. The most prestigious law firms in Washington and New York recruit almost exclusively from Ivy League law schools, the largest investment banks compete for Harvard M.B.A.'s, and the most distinguished medical schools are more likely to admit a Yale graduate than a graduate of, say, Central Michigan University.

But whether this advantage stems directly from four years of Ivy League education or from characteristics that most Ivy League students bring with them to campus or from social connections that students make on campus has never been demonstrated convincingly. Despite a "democratizing" of the Ivy League student body, the bulk of these students come from families in the upper tenth of the U.S. population in terms of economic, social, and political power. Since it still takes a good deal of money to go through professional school, and since jobs with prestige employers still depend to some extent on social connections (and social polish), an Ivy League diploma in itself is less of a guarantee of success than being born to affluent parents who can afford to send their children to an Ivy League campus.

Even the social connections attributed to the Ivy League can be illusory. Like any other aggregate of people, student populations are made up of cliques and crowds, and mere attendance at Harvard or Princeton won't make your child an intimate (or a potential spouse) of the child of a cabinet member, an ambassador, or a Fortune 500 corporate chieftain, even though all of these are enrolled and may even sit next to your child in class.

Is the quality of the education exceptional? Certainly it can be—but this is largely up to the child. Some of the Ivy League faculties include Nobel Laureates and other distinguished scholars and scientists, and the atmosphere is one of intellectual and cultural excitement. (But this is true, also, at the best of the state universities—at the University of California, Berkeley, for example, or the University of Michigan, Ann Arbor. The student at Columbia or Harvard can sit at the feet of a number of world-famous men and women—provided he is motivated to get to their lecture hall. The cultural and political atmosphere—in terms of plays, concerts, visiting lecturers—can be equally stimulating, but not all students participate.

It has been argued that the most important educational feature of any college campus is the intellectual ability of the students, and in this respect the Ivy League, with its stringent selection criteria, is likely to have a distinct advantage over most state universities and small liberal arts colleges. On the other hand, some Ivy League schools are sheltered enclaves for well-to-do students who are bright enough to have gained admission but who are neither motivated nor stimulating.

In terms of costs, full tuition and board for four years at an Ivy League school is likely to be the highest in the country. (Currently it can easily exceed $100,000, and its periodic increases out-strip the inflation rate.) But it's important to recognize that financial aid is also available at rather generous levels because these private schools can rely on their own substantial endowments when federal sources of student assistance shrink. Moreover, because some of them are genuinely concerned with attracting students from a wider range of social, economic, and ethnic backgrounds, many scholarships and other forms of assistance are available for bright students who normally could not consider attending this kind of school.

At some Ivy League campuses, approximately 40% of the students receive some kind of financial assistance.

And so, if your interest in an Ivy League school is shared by your child, and if her academic record predicts that she will profit from the intellectual and cultural advantages, your concerns about costs should not deter her from sending off one of her several applications to a school of this kind.

"We're Looking for a Small Liberal-Arts College"

Many parents—some on the basis of their own campus memories and some on the basis of a popular stereotype—see the small, private liberal-arts college, especially their own alma mater, as the best possible school for their children. But when questioned more closely, these parents come up with a confusing variety of descriptions, because this broad category includes all sorts of institutions—some excellent (and very expensive) and many nondescript (though often not much less expensive).

The small liberal-arts college ranges from such schools as Bennington, Reed, St. John's, and Sarah Lawrence (each with a very distinctive personality as well as astronomical tuition-and-board fees) through such top-grade (and highly selective) schools as Carleton, St. Lawrence, Beloit, and Grinnell, to literally hundreds of institutions with standards ranging from the mediocre to the deplorable, many of them functioning simply as four-year holding tanks for high school graduates with marginal grades and no identifiable interests. But despite the vast differences among them, small colleges have the following virtues—at least in the minds of many parents.

To begin with, the small size of the student body makes it easy for students to make friends with one another and with their instructors. The small class size encourages the faculty to be interested in the individual student. And the faculty, selected for its dedication to teaching rather than to research, is likely to have both the time and the inclination to treat each student as an individual rather than a faceless student number. In addition, because the student body—especially at church-related colleges—is more homogeneous than at a large public institution, the child is less likely to be influenced by (or become romantically involved with) "the wrong kind of classmate." All of this makes the small college especially appealing to parents whose child seems shy or socially immature or fearful about living away from home.

Unfortunately, there is a persuasive set of arguments against each of these idyllic assumptions—and a number of disadvantages to be weighed against them. On the matter of class size, for example, almost every scientifically acceptable study comparing the educational effectiveness of small and large classes finds no difference between them. Along similar lines, studies comparing the classroom effectiveness of "dedicated" teachers and those who are actively involved in research give the edge to the active researchers—presumably on the grounds that the excitement generated by their own research carries over into their classrooms.

The small size of such a college (and its correspondingly low revenues, even if its tuition is high) works to its disadvantage in several ways. Faculty salaries are usually too low to attract the best instructors, and budget restrictions are often reflected in an inadequate library and a very limited program of the cultural activities—concerts, theater, seminars, lectures, and other events—that are an integral part of a liberal education.

These limitations are likely to be most severe in fields involving science and technology. Because sophisticated laboratory and other research facilities are simply beyond the means of the small-scale private college, faculty who are both exciting teachers and active research investigators are unlikely to be attracted, and students interested in any of the scientific fields will have little exposure to state-of-the-art laboratory equipment or state-of-the-art instruction.

The intimacy and homogeneity of the student body, too, has perhaps as many disadvantages as advantages. Spending four years with the same 1,500 students can be stifling, to judge both by the reports of students who stay for all four years and those who transfer, after a year or two, to larger institutions. And if you believe that a crucial part of your child's education involves meeting—and learning to get along with—peers who are very different from him in parental income, place of residence, religion, and ethnicity, the homogeneity of some small colleges will work strongly against this. Experience indicates, too, that the child who wants to "get into trouble" can do so every bit as easily at the small college as the large state university.

"We're Looking for a School that Specializes in—"

If your child's interests, or your ambitions for her, center on a specific career—engineering, for example, or elementary school teaching—you may be looking for a school that specializes or has a strong reputation in the field. The danger here is that at the time of high school graduation, very few students have a balanced notion of their interests and abilities, and even fewer parents or children have a comprehensive view of the whole array of potentially interesting occupations and careers.

As a result, the child may be locked into a career choice that subsequently turns out to be inappropriate or less attractive than alternatives. (Studies show, for example, that high-achieving college students change their major as often as three times during their four undergraduate years.)

This premature commitment need not be damaging if the college you choose exposes the child to available alternatives. If, for example, your child decides on Northwestern University because of its very reputable theater program and then decides that acting is not for him, he can change to another major with no difficulty. Or if he is disappointed in Oberlin's music program, he can still remain in place and get a fine liberal education. But if he goes to a school of technology or a college of education, he will find the curriculum too rigid to allow him to explore alternatives, and he is unlikely to meet either students or faculty who will stimulate his interest in some other career. In such situations, a shift in career choice may require a transfer to another institution—a process that can be costly in terms of both time and money.

"What about the State University?"

A very substantial percentage of students at state universities report that they filed no applications to any other colleges. Although in some cases this may reflect an unawareness of alternatives, in others it signifies a sharp eye for good value.

Like the small liberal arts colleges, state universities range from the stellar to the deplorable, but most of them share certain basic characteristics that distinguish them sharply from most other institutions of higher education.

To begin with, they tend to be large—in terms of both total student body and class size. In part, this size is the consequence of admission standards that are usually less rigorous than those of private schools of equivalent quality. (Some state universities are required by law to admit anyone presenting a high school diploma, but some of these screen out the misfits within the first year.)

Perhaps more important, tuition fees are low—at least for state residents—because the university is subsidized by both state and federal funds. Tuition fees for out-of-state students are significantly higher and climbing rapidly but, if the age of majority in the state is eighteen, an out-of-state student may be able to establish residence on her own within a year or two and qualify for the lower in-state fees.

Because their size provides them with economies of scale, state universities are able to offer a very wide array of programs and courses—from such strictly vocational curriculums as landscape architecture and hotel and restaurant management to such liberal arts subjects as music, philosophy, and history. Some state universities have achieved worldwide reputations in the physical and natural sciences; others have distinguished themselves in the humanities and the social sciences.

In order to serve all areas of their state, a number of states have two or more state universities; other states have established branches of the single state university in several cities and towns. It's important to note that not all state universities in the same state have the same standards, fees, or programs, and this is especially true of the local branches—some of which are nothing more than enlarged teachers' colleges. But it's equally important to recognize that enrolling at a local branch gives an uncertain student an opportunity to try out college at low cost while living at home and then transfer to the main campus if things go well.

The sheer scale of many state universities can intimidate some students. (Each year, at one midwestern state university, a half dozen freshmen from rural areas take one terrified look at the milling throngs involved in the computerized registration process in the vast gymnasium, flee to their dorms, repack their bags, and board the next bus for home.) And class sizes of 50 to 450 students, often taught by graduate assistants rather than full professors, can be off-putting to students accustomed to more personal instruction.

But it can be argued that learning to cope in a vast, impersonal context is valuable preparation for life in an equally vast and impersonal bureaucratic world—and that a young graduate assistant may be far more empathetic to timid freshmen than a middle-aged full professor. In addition, a number of state universities, recognizing the problems caused by size, have established on the main campus several small "cluster" colleges in which students enjoy the intimacy of a smaller group without losing the advantages of a large campus: well-equipped libraries and laboratories, excellent athletic facilities, a rich cultural program, and an extremely diverse student body.

The decision to apply to the state university in your own state depends, of course, on its quality and on your child's social maturity. If the university is a good one, and if your child can tolerate a certain degree of impersonality and is open to new friendships, you may well be getting the best educational bargain available today. A state university in another state may also provide an excellent education, but most of them restrict the enrollment of out-of-state students by imposing higher tuition fees and admission standards.

The Junior or Community College

In order to bring higher education geographically closer to the consumer, a number of states, counties, and local communities have established what are called junior or community colleges. These vary so widely in quality and purpose that it's almost impossible to evaluate them as a group, but an examination of their catalogs—perhaps followed up by a visit—can tell you a good deal about what your own community has to offer.

The best junior colleges are formally linked with the state university. Because both their admission standards and their tuition fees are lower, and because their location permits students to live at home, they are ideal starting points for (1) the student who currently can't afford the considerable cost of going away to college, and (2) the student whose high school record doesn't qualify him, for admission to the main campus. Either type can spend two years at a junior college with minimal investment and then, if his financial situation improves and their performance is good, transfer their credits to the main campus of the state university and finish their four years there.

There are two possible disadvantages of starting out at a junior college of this type: first, if the general level of the student body is somewhat lower than on the main campus, classes may be less stimulating; second, living at home can deprive the student of a social life on campus. But neither of these is inevitable, and both may be a small price to pay for the opportunity to introduce a marginal or reluctant student to college at relatively low cost. Years ago the faculty at junior colleges tended to be inferior to that of the main campus but today, because academic jobs are hard to find, junior colleges are able to hire faculty who are very well qualified.

Some types of junior or community college, however, function not as pipelines to a four-year degree but as post-high-school vocational-training institutions. Offering a two-year "associate degree," they provide training for students interested in becoming computer operators, dental hygienists, X-ray technicians, police officers, and other nonprofessional workers. Admission standards are minimal and fees are low, but the value of the associate degree has been decreasing steadily as the four-year degree has become a virtual requirement for nursing, police work, etc. Even if your child is "not the academic type," the training offered by this kind of community college is likely to have little value, because employment at the nonprofessional level depends far more on the state of the economy than on the qualifications of the individual.

MAKING A CHOICE

First Steps

Although tuition costs, board, and other money matters may be uppermost in your mind, it's a good idea to set them aside during the first stages of choosing a college. The reason is simple: until you've narrowed your choice to two or three schools and investigated all possible sources of financial aid, you can have only the vaguest notion of what your out-of-pocket costs are likely to be.

Another of your worries—Will your child be admitted to "the college of her choice"?—can also be set aside for the moment. This concern may stem from your own college experience, but the situation has changed drastically in the intervening years. A generation ago, when the baby boomers were approaching college age, their sheer number caused many selective colleges to reject as many as five of every six applicants, and the application process was stressful indeed. Today, with the dramatic drop in the teen-aged population, all but the most rigorously selective colleges accept most of their applicants, and there is little question that your child will be admitted if the choices you arrive at are reasonably realistic. His chances of admission to such highly selective schools as Brown or Harvard are not great—no matter how splendid his record—but application to such schools does not involve a large investment. On the other hand, if your child's record is in the respectable range, there is no need to limit your applications to schools with very low standards. These days applicants with decent averages can be certain of being accepted by decent colleges.

The most sensible first step is to sit down with your child and try to reach a decision on the following issues:

- large school or small?
- public or private?
- at home or out of town?—and, if out of town, how far from home?
- how selective?

Once you've reached an agreement (or a compromise), spend a few hours at your public library studying the latest editions of the following books and making a list of possibilities.

> *Barron's Profiles of American Colleges* (Barron's Educational Series, Woodbury, N.Y.). Lists 1,500 accredited colleges including a (not altogether reliable) rating on selectivity.

> *The College Handbook* (College Entrance Examination Board, Princeton, N.J.). Lists 3,100 two- and four-year colleges by state. Describes majors, special programs, and tuition costs.

> Fiske, Edward P., *The Fiske Guide to Colleges* (Times Books, New York). Evaluates several thousand four-year colleges on the basis of self-reporting by college administrators and a selected group of students. As might be expected, the evaluations tend to be positive.

> Fiske, Edward P., *The Fiske Selective Guide to Colleges* (Times Books, New York). Limited to approximately 300 colleges, this book has the same limitations as the preceding entry.

> *Lovejoy's College Guide* (Prentice-Hall, New York). Includes information on tuition, financial aid, and majors.

> Moll, Richard, *The Public Ivys* (Penguin Books, New York). Lists and describes 24 public colleges that most closely resemble the private "Ivy League."

> *Peterson's Annual Guide to Four-Year Colleges* (Peterson's Guides, Princeton). Lists approximately 2,000 colleges along with self-reports on SAT score ranges and selectivity.

Although most of these books include information on costs and financial aid, don't let this influence your initial choices. Instead, use the information to help you decide which colleges seem most suitable regardless of costs. As you learn more about the various sources of financial aid (see p. 135), you may discover that, with luck, you can send your child to a college that you were quite certain you couldn't afford.

The Guidance Counselor

In all of this decision-making, is the high-school college adviser likely to be of help? Possibly—and possibly not. On the one hand, he has a more objective view of your child's academic abilities and a more realistic notion of her chances of admission to a highly selective college. In addition, he may know of local sources of financial aid—scholarships offered by the local women's club or fraternal organization, for example—that won't appear in the guidebooks on financial aid. On the other hand, in order to maintain a good "batting average" in his annual report on "this year's graduates admitted to the college of their choice," he may urge your child to apply to a "safe" but uninteresting school and try to persuade her that it is a fine "choice." And one interesting research study concluded that guidance counselors recommend high-prestige colleges to the children of affluent parents rather than middle-income parents when both were equally qualified academically.

Going on Tour

Although they would not think of buying a car or a boat sight unseen, many parents commit themselves to a college education before they or their child has visited the campus—especially when an admission interview is not required. In terms of what you'll be paying for four years of college, the cost of such a visit is a negligible insurance premium, and it is only by visiting that both you and the child can get a feel for the general social climate of the school.

Although you and your child will probably be offered the standard guided tour of the campus, it's important to let your child go off by himself—to strike up conversations with passing students (and to do some snooping and eavesdropping in the dorms), to sit in on a class in a subject that interests him, and to get a general impression of the make-up and "style" of the student body. Students report that such visits, made thoughtfully and unhurriedly, have "turned them off" at campuses they had admired uncritically from afar and kindled their enthusiasm for some that they hadn't considered seriously.

Filing the Application

Although twenty-five years ago, when admission to college was highly competitive, anxious students filed as many as fifteen or more college applications, the movement from a seller's to a buyer's market should reduce both your anxiety and the number of applications your child sends out. But this should not deter him from submitting several—perhaps five. At least one of these should go to a "high risk" school—that is, one that your child would like to attend if she could get admitted and if you could afford it. Another three might go to desirable schools at which you are reasonably confident about admission and paying the costs. All of these should be accompanied by applications for financial aid—even if you consider yourself only marginally eligible. The fifth application might go to a "last resort" school—one that is a "sure thing" in terms of both admission and costs.

The Final Decision

When the responses arrive—usually in mid-April—you may be tempted to base your choice largely on affordability, especially if one school offers more generous financial aid than the others. But this kind of price comparison can be hazardous to your child's education. One rather mediocre midwestern university, for example, offers a large number of generous supplementary scholarships to winners of the National Merit Scholarship so that its press releases can boast of the large number of such winners in attendance. What is not mentioned in these press releases is that the university also loses a large number of these very bright scholarship recipients who transfer elsewhere within a year or two because of their disappointment with the quality of their courses and their instructors.

It's Not Forever

Almost as traumatic as a rejection from a desirable college is an acceptance at a college whose costs are infinitely beyond your means, even with financial aid. But neither event is as disastrous as it seems at first. You can be fairly confident that one college or another—often one in your own community—will accept your child. Once established there, she can prove herself by earning good grades (which are much more credible to admissions' officers than high school grades) and then apply for a transfer to the college of her choice. If money is the obstacle, there is always the possibility that your financial situation may improve—or that a grandparent or other relative will come to the student's aid. Many students from very poor families started out in junior colleges and achieved so fine a record that they were offered scholarships at four-year colleges and eventually fellowships at professional schools. The local junior college may not be what you or your child had in mind but, as both of you are likely to discover, it's not the end of the world.

But It's Not Over Yet

Once you've paid the first installment for tuition, board, and books, you may be tempted to relax, feeling that the problem is either solved or more or less manageable. But the next four years may see changes in the situation that can continue to affect your budgeting. For one thing, sources of financial aid, many of which are dependent on the federal government, may either expand or shrink after a presidential election. For another, your child may manage to get financial aid once she has enrolled, even though it was withheld initially. Then, too, if your child decides, as many students do, that living in a shared apartment or a co-op house off-campus is cheaper than living and eating in the dorms, your costs may diminish considerably.

On the other hand, if, after a couple of years, your child chooses to major in a professional field—psychology, mathematics, physics, law, or medicine—she will inevitably have to get an advanced degree at a graduate or professional school. If her choice is law or medicine, you may have to prepare yourself for yet another financial burden, because it is virtually impossible for a student to "work her way" through these schools. If, on the other hand, the choice is physics or microbiology or anthropology, the chances are that she will be offered a fellowship that includes a stipend for living costs as well as full tuition. If she is a marginal student, she may not receive this kind of support until she has proved herself, but a year's support is the most that you need plan on.

PAYING FOR COLLEGE

Although the problem of paying for your child's college education may have troubled you, on and off, ever since the child began kicking in the womb, it's possible that you've been exaggerating the problem. It's true, of course, that in recent years college costs have been rising faster than the general cost of living—but this is not true of *all* colleges. It's true that the prospect of writing a check for a year of tuition, room, and board can be staggering—but parents have been thus staggered for decades, and some studies indicate that, allowing for the inflation of incomes as well as college costs, the burden will be no heavier on your budget than it was on your parents' budget when you left home for college. It's true, also, that in recent years the government program of grants and loans for college students has shriveled, but this is likely to change for reasons which few parents consider.

Most parents seem to think that colleges exist exclusively for the benefit of their children—to equip them with the knowledge and the technical and social skills they'll need to qualify for a semiprofessional or professional job. But this child-centered view overlooks the fact that there are two other groups which, although they have no college-age children of their own, are vitally interested in the health of the college system.

The first of these is our society as a whole. It supports colleges, directly and indirectly, because it relies on them to turn out the skilled labor force that is essential for American business and industry. If a system of colleges did not exist, General Motors could, of course, set up an apprenticeship system, recruit promising youngsters in their first year of high school, and turn them into automotive engineers, and IBM could develop computer specialists in the same way. But these and other corporations find it much more economical to take their pick of engineers and computer scientists who have educated themselves at their own expense and their own risk. And so these corporations cheerfully support colleges and universities directly through research grants and other subsidies and indirectly through taxes. And if the supply of skilled labor is threatened by a shortage of college graduates, you may be sure that the government will be heavily pressured to make college more accessible.

A second group vitally interested in college education consists of the colleges themselves. Although they are nonprofit organizations, they could not survive without an adequate supply of customers, and all but the most prestigious of them worry constantly about pricing themselves out of the market. As a consequence, the colleges exert all kinds of pressure—on their own alumni and on the state and federal governments—for gifts, grants, and other subsidies that will keep the cost of an education within the reach of a sufficient number of potential customers. And they offer various forms of financial aid to fill up their classrooms with students who could not afford the full tuition costs.

One visible result of these pressures is that students at state universities pay only about one-third of the actual cost of their education and that only one or two of the most prestigious colleges charge students for their full costs. But more directly important to you is the fact that financial aid—some of it based on need, some on merit—is widely available. And if costs continue to rise more rapidly than parental incomes, you may be sure that increases in the amount of aid will not be far behind.

This doesn't mean that your child, no matter how brilliant his record, can apply confidently to the most expensive of the Ivy League colleges, where costs have skyrocketed to more than $25,000 a year. These colleges can charge high fees because they operate in a seller's market, rejecting many more applicants than they accept. And even though 40% of students at these colleges get some form of financial aid, the tuition may nevertheless be too high for you unless your child is brilliant enough to earn a full scholarship.

But the costs at the more heavily subsidized state universities have not risen as rapidly—especially for state residents—and they average less than one-third of the Ivy League figures. And so, if your child is academically qualified, you will probably be able to manage financially. Certainly the heavy enrollments at the better state universities indicate that many parents with moderate incomes are coping with the problem successfully.

Will the education at a public university be as good as what the best of the private colleges provide? All other things being equal, the quality of a college is only as high as the quality of the students it can attract, and the better state universities are now attracting increasing numbers of excellent students who qualify in every way except financially for the most highly selective private colleges. This influx is undoubtedly making good schools better, and if your own state has a good university system you need have no reservations about it. In addition, state universities usually have more sources of financial aid and more sophisticated advisers for students who need it.

At almost every major college, applications for admission and applications for financial aid are considered independently. Thus, your child may be admitted but her application for financial aid may be rejected. But this should not deter you from applying to an expensive but desirable college, because other sources of aid may be available.

Sources of Aid

The difficulties that many parents and students experience in getting financial aid are due less to the lack of aid than to their lack of information about where to find it and how to apply for it. Few high school guidance counselors are fully informed about sources of aid, and those who are conscientious about it find themselves faced with a situation that changes constantly as government programs are canceled or modified. For the same reasons, various handbooks and guides to financial aid, even those that are revised annually, are to some extent out of date on the day they are published. Nevertheless, if you are both aggressive and persistent, you can find information from the sources we describe below.

Your Own Resources Since any application for a scholarship or other financial aid will require you to list details about your income and your family budget, you may just as well begin the search process with a careful calculation of the maximum out-of-pocket contribution you can make toward your child's first year of college expenses. There is no point in calculating on a four-year basis because the financial aid prospects may improve once your child has proved herself or, on the other hand, she may decide that college is not for her.

Just how far this sum will go toward covering all costs depends, of course, on the college you finally choose, the aid your child can get, and your child's "standard of living," but in any event you'll need this figure as a starting point. Bear in mind that you won't need the money in a lump sum. College tuition and board fees can be paid in installments, and payments for books, supplies, and incidentals will also be spaced out across the academic year.

If you've been successful in building a nest egg—in the form of your own investments or a custodial account for the child—now is the time to use it, because the yield on it that you sacrifice is likely to be lower than even the most favorable loan interest. And, of course, funds in a custodial account are legally usable for college tuition regardless of the child's age. Lacking this kind of nest egg, you may be able to ask the child's grand-parents for help in the form of a gift or a loan, or you may be able to get a home equity loan, but it's best to consider these sources as a last resort, because listing them on an application for financial aid will lower your chances of getting it.

If you think that your resources consist only of the money that you've been able to put together, you may be overlooking another important resource: your child's high school record and other qualifications. Your money will, of course, be used to meet the costs, but the costs themselves will be determined by your child's likelihood of winning some kind of scholarship.

Scholarships Although the descriptions of most scholarships stress that some are awarded for merit and others on the basis of need, this information can be misleading in two ways. First, needy students who do not show distinct promise will not get a need-based scholarship. Second, "needy" is not a synonym of "poor"; a family with a gross income considerably above the national average may be considered needy if it has unusually high medical costs, several children in college simultaneously, or other unusually high expenses and obligations. Unless you are clearly affluent, then, you should not be deterred from applying for need-based scholarships, because currently these are more numerous than those based on merit.

The most widely publicized scholarships based on merit are the National Merit Scholarships. Unfortunately, so much media attention is concentrated on the 2,000 top winners that few people realize that the total number of awards runs to about 6,500. These scholarships, for runners-up, are awarded by individual colleges and by major corporations (mainly for children of their own employees). The amounts vary, depending in some cases on the student's financial need, but some colleges are willing to supplement these scholarships with their own funds in order to attract promising students to their campuses. The National Merit Scholarships is one program on which your child's guidance counselor has full information, but it is important to note that to be eligible students must take the Preliminary Scholastic Aptitude Test in their junior year at high school.

Many major corporations award scholarships, some to the children of their own employees, others to students in the local community, still others to any college applicant. In addition, some veterans' organizations, church groups, and fraternal organizations offer scholarships ranging from $100 to several thousand dollars, although these may have some eligibility restrictions attached: some may require that the recipients be children of veterans or members of a specific religious or ethnic group, or that the money be used for study in a specified field. Some are awarded outright, others on the basis of competition among eligible applicants.

Many colleges themselves offer full or partial scholarships—for academic as well as athletic promise, although public attention seems focused almost exclusively on the latter. Some of these academic scholarships are intended to supplement the partial National Merit Scholarships awarded to runners-up, and some are restricted to the children of alumni, but others are more widely available.

Although the offer of a scholarship can be very gratifying, some offers need to be approached with caution. Athletic scholarships are, of course, notoriously dangerous, especially in connection with basketball, football, and other popular spectator sports. In return for the scholarship, the recipient literally sells his services as a revenue-producing performer to the college, and his practice and travel obligations virtually monopolize time that should be devoted to classwork and study. The grade records and graduation rates of scholarship athletes is dismal, not because the recipients are "dumb jocks" but because their team obligations make good academic work nearly impossible. And the number of scholarship athletes who go on to successful professional athletic careers is exceedingly small. Tempting as they are, athletic scholarships of this sort should be avoided.

Oddly enough, even some academic scholarships need to be scrutinized carefully. A number of second-rate private colleges, eager to bolster faltering enrollments or to attract competent students, offer seemingly generous scholarships, but before deciding that such an offer is an educational bargain you would do well to check out the college in one of the sources listed on page 130.

Grants and Loans Before applying for any kind of personal or home-equity loan, you should check the possibility that your child may be eligible for one of the several federal assistance programs. Some of these provide outright, nonrepayable grants; others guarantee low-interest loans made to the student, with repayment delayed until graduation. Some are based on need as measured by your child's Student Aid Index, but others are available almost without regard to family income.

Among the financial aid programs currently functioning are the following:

Pell Grants, in amounts up to $3,600 a year, are based on financial need and college costs. They are available to part-time as well as full-time students, and they need not be repaid.

Supplemental Educational Opportunity Grants (SEOG), offering as much as $4,000 a year, give priority to recipients of Pell Grants. They are awarded on the basis of financial need, the availability of SEOG money at the particular college, and the amount of other financial aid available to the applicant. Like Pell Grants, they need not be repaid.

Perkins Loans (formerly NDSL, or National Direct Student Loans) are available to both undergraduate and graduate students, to a maximum of $9,000 for four years. They must be repaid, with an interest rate of 5%.

Stafford Loans, which have replaced the Guaranteed Student Loans, are made by commercial lenders. The interest rate is 8% for the first four years and 10% thereafter. The amount that can be borrowed annually increases as the student progresses through college, with a maximum of $17,250 for undergraduates.

Federal College Work-Study Program is a federally funded program that pays students (at close to the minimum wage) for work done for the college. The program takes into consideration the student's financial need as well as his or her course workload. Although some of the jobs are menial, some students have found new interests or a new career through working for faculty members or a specific department.

PLUS Loans, unlike Guaranteed Student Loans, may be made to either parents or students and no need-based test is involved, but interest rates are higher and repayment schedules far less lenient.

State Grants and Loans. Many of the states have established educational assistance programs that provide grants to college students, but the amount of money available varies from year to year. Some of these are usable only at public colleges within the state; others are somewhat more liberal. Currently, for example, North Carolina will lend qualified students $5,000 a year for four years and waive the entire principal if, on graduation, the student teaches for a certain ·length of time in a public school.

Because both the funding available for these programs and their eligibility requirements change from time to time, we cannot describe each of them in detail here. But if your child's guidance counselor does not have up-to-date information you can consult the most recent editions of the following books in your local library. (Some of them are published annually or biennially.) Not all of them are likely to be available, but there is considerable overlap in their coverage.

Blum, Laurie, *Free Money for College* (Facts On File).

Cassidy, Daniel J., *The Scholarship Book* (Prentice-Hall, Princeton, N.J.).

The College Board, *The College Cost Book* (College Entrance Examination Board, New York).

College Financial Aid Annual (Simon & Schuster, New York).

Directory of Financial Aid for Minorities (Reference Service Press, San Carlos, Calif.).

Jaffe, David, *The New College Financial Aid System* (Council Oaks Books, Tulsa, Okla.)

Kirby, Debra, *Fund Your Way through College* (Visible Ink, Detroit).

Paying Less for College (Peterson's Guides, Princeton, N.J.).

Peterson's College Money Handbook (Peterson's Guides, Princeton, N.J.).

Rosenwasser, Edward, *How to Obtain Maximum Financial Aid* (Student College Aid, Houston).

On-Campus Jobs

Although "working your way through college" does not actively improve a student's character or academic performance, a moderate work schedule—of no more than 20 hours a week—is likely to do no harm to either. Students whose studies are most likely to suffer from working are those who take on virtually full-time jobs—such as clerking on the night shift at a motel—and catch up on their sleep in class.

Many of the jobs on campus and in the surrounding community—bussing tables in a campus dining hall, for example, or clerking in a nearby bookstore—are available to anyone, but the more interesting jobs, in the college libraries, teaching departments, and research laboratories, are usually restricted to participants in the Federal College Work-Study Program. Because this program subsidizes the wages of the student workers, the employers pay less for their labor and the student earns at least the minimum wage for work that may stimulate or enrich his own academic interests. Eligibility is restricted to students who can demonstrate financial need and who have the requisite skills.

Your Child's Standard of Living

No matter what the tuition costs of the college you finally choose, your total costs will depend very heavily on how your child lives on campus and what he considers himself entitled to. Is he willing, for example, to save one-third to one-half of the substantial cost of textbooks by buying used copies instead of new ones or by sharing an expensive one with a roommate? If his meals are provided for a fixed fee in the dining hall, is he willing to turn down a roommate's invitation to skip dinner and go to a restaurant instead? Will your daughter feel like an outcast if she can't buy the newest fashion in sneakers or the latest CD? And how often will your child want to come home if the trip involves a $400 airline ticket?

Students with far less spending money than their classmates don't always have an easy time of it, but many of them survive with a fine education and perhaps a heightened social sensitivity. Students who insist on keeping up with the Joneses in their dorm don't necessarily get a good education but they cost their parents a great deal more.

Child or Adult?

With 18 as the legal age of majority, your child is almost certain to become an adult before completing four years of college. Although this frees you from any obligation to meet his or her expenses, you are unlikely to take advantage of this opportunity. You should not, however, overlook some advantages that it offers.

For one thing, an adult can establish independent residence and thus avoid paying out-of-state tuition fees at a desirable university. For another, his or her income (which is likely to be minimal) can qualify him for student aid not available when he is supported by you. And, if necessary, he or she may be able to qualify for food stamps.

Part III

SOME SPECIAL
SITUATIONS

Parts I and II, which were arranged in roughly chrono-logical sequence, dealt with financial issues that concern almost every parent, and the age of your child probably determined which of the chapters attracted your closest attention.

Most of the chapters in Part III, in contrast, deal with special problems that do not affect all parents and that may arise at almost any point in the child's life. The problems of providing financial security for a handicapped child (Chapter 10), for example, affect only a small minority of parents. Methods of helping your adult child financially (Chapter 9) may not interest you for many years to come. Even the ways of handling the child's income tax return (Chapter 8) and planning your own estate (Chapter 11) may not concern you until both you and your child are older or more affluent than you are right now.

For this reason, Part III can best be used as a reference tool. As in a dictionary or an encyclopedia, its "entries" bear no relationship to one another, and each is likely to interest different groups of readers at different stages of their lives.

CHAPTER 7

CHILD SUPPORT AFTER
DIVORCE, SEPARATION, OR
ABANDONMENT

Ideally, divorce or separation, whatever its emotional impact on the couple's children, should have little effect on their standard of living. A child-support agreement properly negotiated and drafted and faithfully complied with should provide the custodial parent with enough money to pay for the child's support and other normal expenses.

Unfortunately, this ideal situation prevails only rarely in real life. Most custodial parents—usually the mother—find that after divorce or separation both their income and standard of living drop alarmingly, not only because their own earnings are low but because child-support orders are violated. Their child's father, having acquired a new wife and perhaps some stepchildren, is either unable to support two households or simply loses interest in contributing to the support of his own children. Support payments, which may have been inadequate to begin with, become sporadic or stop altogether, leaving the mother to cope with a truly desperate situation. As a result, increasing numbers of women who formerly regarded themselves as solidly middle-class find themselves in the ignominious position of having to apply for welfare.

Recognizing their plight, Congress, in 1984, enacted the Child Support Enforcement Amendments, which attempted to alleviate the situation through a number of legislative changes and innovations, among them the following:

> Under threat of losing its federal funding for its welfare program, each state is required to establish an office of Child Support Enforcement and a Parent Locator Service whose functions are to trace delinquent fathers and force them to fulfill their financial obligations to their children. These agencies were empowered to act swiftly, often without the need for time-consuming judicial authorization or review.
>
> A Federal Office of Child Support Enforcement and a Federal Parent Locator Service were established to supplement their state counterparts when divorced parents no longer live in the same state.
>
> The Uniform Reciprocal Enforcement of Support Act, now adopted by all states, requires states to cooperate with one another in the enforcement and collection of child-support payments.

Many requirements of the 1984 amendments were strengthened through Congressional passage of the Family Support Act of 1988. As a result of federal law, and implementing state legislation, each state now provides for presumptive support guidelines, establishment of parentage at least until a child's eighteenth birthday, genetic testing for purposes of determining parentage, medical support, support enforcement through income withholding, imposition of liens on real and *personal property* owned by the obligated parents, the posting of bonds to ensure support payment, and expedited processes for child support actions.

The Child Support Recovery Act of 1992 made it a federal crime to willfully fail to pay a past due support obligation with respect to a child who resides in another state. A past due support obligation is an amount due under court order or administrative process that exceeds $5,000 or has remained unpaid for longer than a year. The Act's most far-reaching impact, however, may result from the creation of a Commission on Child and Family Welfare, which has many duties related to child custody, visitation, domestic violence, and children in the foster and family court systems.

Because the effectiveness of these laws varies considerably between one state and another, they are unlikely to provide a panacea, but preliminary evaluations indicate that they do, in fact, provide divorced, separated, or abandoned mothers with some help in collecting child-support payments—provided that these mothers live in a state that has developed an effective system and are able to cope with a sometimes frustrating bureaucracy. But in any state mothers are likely to get prompter and more effective help if they have a clear understanding of their legal rights and how to enforce them.

Recently a number of private for-profit organizations have been established to function essentially as collection agencies, tracking down delinquent fathers and enforcing support orders. These organizations charge their claimants as much as one-third of the amount they collect, and opportunities for fraud are rather obvious, but some successful claimants point out that collecting 66% of what is owed them "is a lot better than nothing," and some overburdened state support-enforcement agencies have enlisted the help of these private groups.

PARENTAL OBLIGATIONS

Under the common law, parents are obligated to support their children until the age of majority unless the children marry earlier, join the military service, or are "emancipated" by court order. The standard of living provided for the children will, of course, vary with the family's income, and the law will not intervene unless there is clear evidence of deprivation or neglect.

Primary responsibility for this support falls on the biological or adoptive father. Under the common law, he has full responsibility for the support of his children even if the mother or the children have sufficient assets to make them self-supporting. This support must continue after separation unless the child left the father's home for no legally satisfactory reason (e.g., the child ran away); in such a situation the father is not obligated to provide support if he is willing to take his child back and support him under his own roof.

Fathers must provide for the child's support regardless of where or with whom the child actually lives. The father of a child in the custody of a divorced wife remains responsible for the child's support, as does the identified father of an illegitimate child, whether or not he lives with the child. If a severely handicapped child is housed in a state institution, or if a child is supported by a social agency, the father can be required to reimburse the government for its expenses or outlays—at least until the child attains majority, and in some states beyond majority.

Generally the mother's responsibility for support of the children is secondary to that of the father and comes into play only if the father is dead, missing, or incapable of providing support. But some state laws hold the mother and father equally responsible. This does not mean that each must contribute the same dollar amount but rather that each must share the support responsibility in proportion to his/her income and other circumstances.

A man's obligation to support his stepchildren is governed by state law. Some states impose this responsibility if the children live with him. In other states, the children may be entitled to welfare if neither their natural father nor their stepfather is contributing to their support.

Although a father's obligation to support a child ends as soon as the child reaches the age of majority, marries, enters military service, or is emancipated by court order, child-support orders in a few states require the father to contribute to the full costs of a college education or to continue his support as long as the child is a full-time student. In addition, the laws of some states require a father to support indefinitely a child who is too severely handicapped to be able to earn a living. State law may also require parents to reimburse a state institution for an adult child's custodial care although payments are usually based on the parents' income level rather than actual costs.

The foregoing principles, some of which date back several decades, have been modified by two relatively recent changes: the influx of mothers into the labor force and the more frequent awarding of child custody to the father rather than the mother. States differ in the extent to which they recognize these changes, but some courts, in formulating a support order, take into account the earnings of the mother. Paternal custody, on the other hand, has been so rare that few general legal principles governing such support have evolved, although in some cases a noncustodial mother has been ordered to make support payments.

THE ROLE OF THE STATE

Although both the common law and most state modifications of it are intended to provide the child of divorced parents with a measure of security, they have often proved ineffective because, until recently, they could be, and were, violated with impunity. Fathers who lost interest in supporting their children, or who believed that their support payments were unjustified, unnecessary, or excessive, or who felt that the child's mother was not respecting their visitation rights, simply stopped paying, and there was virtually nothing that the custodial mother could do to compel payment. Other fathers abandoned their families and disappeared before or after any support order had been formulated.

The Child Support Enforcement Offices, established in 1984, can help abandoned and divorced women with any or all of the following procedures:

- establishing the father's paternity
- locating a missing father
- obtaining enforceable support orders
- monitoring or enforcing support payments

The services of a state Child Support Enforcement Office are available to all, regardless of income. Mothers receiving welfare payments are required to use the services, and any moneys collected by the agency must be used to reimburse the state for welfare payments. Other women may be charged a nominal fee based on income. There may, in addition, be expenses for collection of the payments, but in some states these are charged to the supporting father rather than the custodial parent.

Because the Child Support Enforcement Office is primarily a collection agency, it does not deal with other potential sources of conflict: visitation rights, property division, or custody. But despite these limitations, women who have experienced frustration and failure in their attempts to obtain child support see it as a potentially invaluable source of help.

Establishing Paternity

Establishing the child's paternity not only fixes responsibility for support payments but also gives the child other advantages: the right to inherit from the father, eligibility for the father's health insurance and Social Security benefits, and the opportunity to enhance her sense of identity by establishing a relationship with the "other half" of her parentage. Paternity should be established even if the father is a penniless teenager, because he may be able—and will be obligated—to support the child in later years.

The state Child Support Enforcement Office—assisted by county courts, if necessary—can help abandoned mothers to establish paternity. To initiate the process, the mother must provide the agency staff with whatever evidence she can muster to support her claim: the alleged father's letters or gifts to the child, evidence of his earlier financial support, photographs of him with the child, testimony of friends as to his relationship with the mother. Once this evidence is at hand, a formal complaint can be filed against the alleged father.

If the alleged father fails to respond, the court can establish his paternity by default and issue an order for child support that is enforceable nationwide. If the alleged father does respond but denies paternity or is uncertain about it, the Child Support Enforcement Office can require him to submit to blood tests. These tests are accurate enough to exclude 99% of wrongfully accused men and to indicate a high probability of his paternity if he is not excluded.

Actually, very few legitimate paternity claims go to trial. Confronted with persuasive evidence and with the threat of further legal action, most fathers acknowledge paternity. In this event, the mother and father, perhaps with the help of a staff member of the Child Support Enforcement Office, can draft a consent court order specifying the level and schedule of support payments. In most states, this order must be approved by a local family or domestic court, which may add to it precise arrangements for custody, visitation, health insurance, and other parental rights and obligations. If a consent order cannot be negotiated, either parent can request a formal hearing, after which the court will determine paternity, establish the support obligation, and specify its terms in a court order.

Establishing paternity when the alleged father is living in another state is likely to be more difficult and time-consuming. Although the Uniform Reciprocal Enforcement of Support Act (URESA) has made interstate cooperation easier, each state nevertheless has its own paternity laws, and if a court trial becomes necessary it must be held in the alleged father's state of residence.

Locating the Father

The issues of paternity and collecting support are, of course, irrelevant if the father, alleged or admitted, can't be found, because, until he is located, he can't be served with notice of any legal action pending against him or brought before a judge. In its efforts to locate the missing father, the success of the Child Support Enforcement Office depends very heavily on information provided by the mother. If she believes that the missing father is living in the local area, the following kinds of information can be useful:

- the father's Social Security number and last known address
- name and address of the father's current or most recent employer
- names and addresses of friends or relatives

- local creditors, such as banks, utility companies, or department stores; organizations to which he belongs; or places where he has been known to spend leisure time.

The Child Support Enforcement Office, because it is a government agency, may have access to "confidential" information that would otherwise be withheld from the mother as a private citizen. This governmental power becomes especially significant if the father has left the local community. In such an event, if the mother can provide, in addition to his name, the father's Social Security number—which may be found on old bank statements, income tax returns, pay-check stubs, hospital records, and similar documents—the State Parent Locator Service can search for an address in the records of the department of motor vehicles, the state tax department, correctional facilities, and other state agencies.

If the father cannot be found within the state, the Federal Parent Locator Service can use its powerful resources to continue the search nationwide. Furnished with the father's name and Social Security number, this agency can search the records of every federal agency, including the IRS—whose records are not legally accessible to anyone for any other purpose. The Federal Parent Locator Service will report its findings—perhaps including the father's current income—to the local Child Support Enforcement Office.

The Child Support Order

In order to collect child support, you will need a legally enforceable court order that sets the amount and terms of payment. Child support orders are issued by judges, either to formalize an agreement negotiated by the parents or to reflect the judge's decision after hearing evidence from both sides. The order may result from any of several types of situations: a divorce or legal separation, an independent action for child support, a paternity case, a child-abandonment case, or a URESA support action. Whatever the situation, the judge is primarily concerned with fairness to both parties, the welfare of the child, and the enforceability of the order.

Although states—and individual judges—vary widely in determining the amount of the support payments, they generally take the position that the divorced father's remarriage and acquisition of a second family does not relieve him of his support obligations. With this basic premise, the courts generally take into account the following factors:

- the needs of the child
- the current and potential earnings of each parent
- other assets and sources of parental income
- the number of dependents and other debts and obligations of the supporting parent
- the general standard of living of each parent
- alternatives to cash payments—the possibility, for example, that in lieu of support payments for medical expenses, the child could be covered under the father's health insurance plan.

Determining Financial Need

In most states, the amount of child support is determined by balancing the needs of the children against the financial ability of the noncustodial parent. But custodial parents often find the amount insufficient simply because they have failed to make an accurate estimate of their actual costs. Prior to any negotiation session or hearing, therefore, it is very important to prepare a realistic budget.

This may be difficult for several reasons. If, prior to the divorce, you played the role of housewife, relegating the payment of bills entirely to your husband, you may not have an accurate notion of the costs of running a household. And if you are about to take on paid employment, you may not foresee the costs of child care, transportation, and lunches. If you have been subsisting without support for some time, you may have become accustomed to a bare-bones budget. On the other hand, if you list actual costs realistically, you may fear being criticized for extravagance.

The lawyer or social worker handling your case will probably provide you with a budget form to fill out. This can be helpful, but you may still overlook substantial costs that recur infrequently: real estate and other taxes, seasonal clothing costs, summer camp fees, medical costs. It is important, too, to include things that your child really needs even though you have not been able to provide them without support from the custodial parent.

In determining the level of child support, many states use standardized charts which establish the monthly cost of various goods and services the child typically needs. Although these charts can be helpful in reducing possible bias in the court system and in providing a basis for out-of-court settlements, they have a number of limitations.

To begin with, the standard of living they reflect is extremely low, and generally they do not take full acccount of household costs, assuming that they will be paid where they are incurred—that is, by the custodial parent. Moreover, because they are formulated for the "typical" situation, they may not include expenses that are genuine but atypical: ongoing medical costs for a child with a chronic illness, for example, or special instruction for a child who is gifted.

Perhaps more important, many courts apply these charts on a "cost-sharing" basis: that is, if both parents earn essentially the same income, each will be required to contribute half the costs. Such a policy overlooks the unremunerated work of the custodial parent in running the household and caring for the child. But even if this unpaid work is disregarded, support payments are usually inequitable. Although government reports in 1989 estimated the annual cost of rearing a child as $12,056, the average child support payable to mothers in 1989 was only $2,295.

Critics of the cost-sharing approach prefer what is called an "income-equalization" approach. Instead of attempting to isolate the direct child-rearing costs from general household costs, this method uses government standard-of-living figures to determine overall costs for the family unit and then allocates the incomes of both parents in an attempt to meet this figure.

Whatever the level of payments set by court order, it is not necessarily permanent, since both circumstances and earnings are likely to change over time. The mother may remarry, or her earnings may improve—or she may be faced with unexpected expenses for her child. The supporting father may experience business reverses or incur other obligations—or he may find himself far more affluent than he anticipated. In any of these events, either parent can petition the court for a change in the level of support payments or other terms of the order, although the other parent must be notified of the petition and given the opportunity to contest the proposed change.

Enforcement of Payments

A support order entered by the court is legally enforceable, but this in itself does not guarantee that payments will be made as specified. Like other court orders, it can be violated. But the ability of the mother to enforce ordered payments has been enhanced by the establishment of the Child Support Enforcement Office.

Once the support order has been entered by the court, the Child Support Enforcement Office may serve as the actual collector—recording payments received and reminding the obligated father if his payments are late. This service may be mandatory for women on the welfare rolls, but it may also be available to others.

Although state Child Support Enforcement Offices vary in the measures they use to enforce support orders and in the vigor with which they use them, all of the following have been authorized, and many of them have been highly effective.

Liens A lien placed on property owned by the father—a house, for example, or a boat or a vehicle—is simply evidence that a creditor has a claim to that property and it does not in itself produce cash payment. But because the property can't be sold while it is thus encumbered, the defaulting father may be induced to remove the lien by making support payments.

Seizure of Personal Property In some states, the Child Support Enforcement Office has the right to order anyone holding property that belongs to a defaulting father—money in a bank account, for example, or securities in the hands of a stockbroker—to withhold the property from its owner and deliver it in satisfaction of the child-support payments. In some states, any personal property belonging to a defaulting father may be attached and sold for the same purpose.

Wage Withholding The Child Support Enforcement Office is required to impose automatic wage withholding on any father whose support payments are in arrears 30 days or more, and employers are required to comply with such an order. Although there are limits on the amount that can be withheld from each payroll check, the proceeds can be used not only for current support but also for payment of arrears. All new support orders and all modifications of existing ones must contain a provision for wage withholding so that the mother can, if she prefers, take full advantage of wage withholding as a collection method.

The withholding of wages is not restricted to private employment. The wages and pensions of military personnel and civil service employees may also be withheld, and so may unemployment compensation and any other state or federal benefits if the father is jobless.

Tax Refunds Both state and federal governments are authorized to divert to the payment of child-support any income-tax refunds to which a defaulting father is entitled. All that is required is the filing of a claim by the Child Support Enforcement Office.

EXPECTATIONS VS. REALITY

In 1989, 5 million out of 10 million women with children from absent fathers were awarded child support. Of these 5 million 25% received nothing, and only 51% received the full amounts awarded.

Although there seems little doubt that the several agencies and the new regulations established by the 1984 Child Support Enforcement Amendments have great potential for helping women arrange for and collect child support, a reading of this chapter should not generate excessive optimism.

To begin with, federally mandated programs which look dazzlingly promising as formulated by Congress often undergo a dramatic change of complexion when they are implemented by states with inadequate budgets or unsympathetic legislatures. In short, the actual performance of a particular Child Support Enforcement Office may bear little resemblance to what we have described here.

Even if the various agencies perform perfectly, however, they may not be able to produce the promised results. Fathers fleeing family responsibilities are not above changing their names, moving frequently, and employing other means to avoid paying child support.

Judges, too, often disappoint mothers by setting a level of support payments that seems inadequate. On the one hand, judges, who are predominantly male, may show excessive sympathy for the absent father. On the other hand, it is also possible that the level of support insisted upon by the mother is based as much on vindictiveness against the father as on the realistic needs of her child.

In general, then, although mothers should try to use every resource that promises aid in obtaining child support, they should not allow this to preoccupy them to the exclusion of the broader recommendations and suggestions offered in the earlier chapters of this book.

C H A P T E R 8

YOUR CHILD AND THE GOVERNMENT: TAXES AND BENEFITS

In their attitudes toward the government, many Americans show a curious ambivalence. Faced with filing their income-tax returns, they often feel strong resentment or hostility toward the IRS in particular and toward the government in general. But when circumstances force them to take advantage of such tax-supported services as unemployment insurance, food stamps, welfare payments, or Medicaid, they often turn this hostility toward themselves, losing their self-respect and feeling ashamed or worthless.

Neither of these feelings is rational or productive. Americans are taxed at a far lower rate than the citizens of any comparable modern society and, although we may resent some of the budget items on which our taxes are spent, vindictiveness toward the IRS, or daredevil tactics to reduce our tax bill, are not effective ways of changing government priorities. Shame about seeking government help, on the other hand, can be downright self-destructive. Low-income parents of young children who, out of fear of becoming "welfare bums," struggle to survive "on their own" rather than accepting "government handouts" show little responsibility toward their children by rejecting help which they may need desperately and to which they are thoroughly entitled.

Our discussion of taxes is based on three premises: (1) that taxes are inevitable; (2) that every legitimate means of lowering our tax bill should be used but that "creative" tax-reducing tactics are likely to be ineffective if not downright dangerous; and (3) that all financial decisions should be based on their fundamental soundness rather than their tax consequences. It is all too easy for an investor to cut off his financial nose to spite the IRS.

Similarly, our discussion of government benefits stems from our assumption that those who need these forms of social insurance are fully entitled to them, having paid their premiums in the form of taxes—and that feelings of shame are inappropriate, because their economic plight is in no way their own fault.

FEDERAL INCOME TAX

Claiming Your Child as a Dependent

A dependency exemption for your child can first be claimed on your tax return for the year of his birth, even if he was born on December 31. Claims involving a step-, foster, or adopted child begin with the year in which the relationship was established. The amount of the dependency exemption is the same as the personal exemption ($2,350 for 1993).

Five conditions must be met before an exemption for a dependent is allowed:

1. The claimed dependent must have less than $2,300 of gross income for the calendar year in which the tax year of the taxpayer begins, except where the dependent is a child of the taxpayer and either is under age 19 at the close of such calendar year or is a full-time student under age 24 at the end of the calendar year, although special rules apply to students age 24 or over;
2. More than half of the dependent's total support for that calendar year must have been furnished by the taxpayer (with exceptions relating to multiple support agreements and children of divorced parents);
3. The dependent must be a child, grandchild, stepchild, adopted child, or one of the several other relationships allowed by the IRS;
4. The dependent must not have filed a joint return with his spouse; and

5. The dependent must be a citizen, national, or resident of the United States, a resident of Canada or Mexico, or an alien child adopted by and living with a U.S. citizen or national as a member of his household for the entire tax year.

It's essential to recognize that only *one* person (or *one* joint return) can claim any one child as a dependent. Generally, the dependency exemption for children of divorced taxpayers will go to the parent who has custody of the child for the greater part of the calendar year. This rule applies only if the child receives over one-half of his or her support from the parents who are divorced or legally separated, or have lived apart for the last six months of the calendar year. In addition, the child must have been in the custody of one or both parents for more than one-half of the calendar year.

There are three exceptions to the rule that a custodial parent is entitled to the dependency exemption: (1) when there is a multiple support agreement that allows the child to be claimed as a dependent by a taxpayer other than the custodial parent; (2) when the custodial parent releases his or her right to the child's dependency exemption to the noncustodial parent (This release must be executed in writing [using IRS form 8332] and attached to the noncustodial parent's tax return for each year the exemption is released.) and (3) when a pre-1985 divorce decree between the parents grants the exemption to the noncustodial parent and the noncustodial parent provides at least $600 for the support of the child for the year in question.

In all situations that are in any way atypical, records must be kept very carefully, because many taxpayers who in good faith have supported a dependent have had their exemptions disallowed because they could not substantiate them.

Child-Care Tax Credit

If you and your spouse are employed, and if you pay someone to care for your child who is under the age of 15 or is handicapped, you may claim a tax credit on your federal income-tax return. The eligibility requirements are a bit complex, but they are worth examining, because a tax *credit* is worth far more than an exemption or a deduction. An exemption for a dependent, for example, merely reduces the amount of your taxable income. A credit, on the other hand, is subtracted directly from the tax itself.

If you are married, you and your spouse can claim the child-care credit provided:

- You pay for certain types of child care (see p. 68)
- You and your spouse are employed for wages full-time or part-time unless one of you is a full-time student or incapacitated
- You maintain a household in which the child lives
- You file a joint tax return unless you are separated.

If you are separated, divorced, or unmarried, you can claim the child-care credit provided:

- You maintain a household in which your child lives for more than half of the year
- You contribute more than half of the cost of maintaining the household for a full year
- Your spouse was not a member of the household during the last six months of the tax year
- You file an individual tax return.

If you are unmarried, separated, or divorced, you can claim the credit for the care of the child even if someone else is claiming the dependency exemption provided that you have custody of the child for more than half of the tax year.

The amount of the credit you can claim is based on adjusted gross income. With an income of $10,000 or less, you can claim 30% of your actual costs up to a maximum of $2,400 for one child and $4,800 for two or more. For adjusted gross incomes of more than $10,000 the 30% credit is reduced by 1% for each $2,000 or fraction thereof, but this reduction ends when the 20% level is reached—at $28,000.

Your Child's Tax Return

A dependent child must file an income-tax return for any year in which his or her income includes either of the following:

- Unearned income (from interest, dividends, etc.) of $600 or more (for 1993).
- Earned income (from wages and self-employment, e.g., baby-sitting, lawn-mowing, etc.) of more than $3,700 (for 1993).

A child whose income does not exceed these limits may nevertheless need to file a return in order to get a refund of taxes withheld from wages, but full-time students who work part-time for low wages may be able to claim exemption from withholding.

A child is taxable on his or her income, including wages, income from property, and trust income. No exemption is allowed for a child eligible to be claimed as a dependent on another taxpayer's return. The basic standard deduction for such dependents is limited to the greater of $600 (for 1993) or the amount of earned income up to the regular standard deduction (generally $ 3,700). A dependent child who is not allowed his or her own exemption and who realizes gross income not exceeding $600 will not be taxable on that amount and need not file a tax return.

In 1993 the tax rate for a single individual was 15% on taxable income up to $22,100, and 28% on income between $22,100 and $53,500. If a minor fails to pay income tax when due, his parents are liable for taxes on the child's salary or wages.

In order to file an income-tax return, the child must have a Social Security number (see p. 55), but the phrase "applied for" may be written on the form in place of the number if it has not been obtained by the time the return is due. If the child is unable to sign the return, the parent or guardian should sign the child's name followed by the phrase "by [signature] parent (or guardian) of minor."

If a child under the age of 14 had no earned income, received unearned income of more than $500 but less than $5,000, and made no estimated tax payments, his parents may elect to report the income on their own return. In such circumstances, the child need not file a return.

Using the Child as a Tax Shelter

Because your child's income-tax bracket is likely to be lower than yours throughout his childhood, you may be tempted to reduce your own tax bill by shifting certain income-producing assets from your name to his. In other chapters we discuss the use of custodial accounts (see p. 55), gifts (see p. 170), and trusts (see pp. 53, 58), as devices for doing this. There is no question that judicious use of these strategies can produce some perfectly legitimate tax reductions for you, but since each of them involves your permanent loss of control over the assets, you need to determine very carefully whether the tax saving is worth this price or whether you are motivated merely to frustrate the IRS.

Moreover, the saving effected by shifting income to the child's lower bracket has been reduced by the Tax Reform Act of 1986, which requires a child's unearned income above $1,200 per year to be taxed at the parents' rate until the child reaches age fourteen.

Another method of lowering your own tax bill can be used if you operate a business or profession of some sort. If you hire your child as a bona fide employee, her wages are tax-deductible by you and taxable for her—presumably at a lower rate if at all. But this arrangement with your child must be every bit as formal as it would be with a stranger. Wages must actually be paid, and demonstrable services, whether full-time, part-time, or seasonal, must be rendered on a scheduled basis. You will not be allowed a tax deduction simply because your child "helped out" in your office or store now and then without receiving actual wages.

GOVERNMENT BENEFITS

Programs of government assistance fall into two categories: those for which everyone is eligible under certain circumstances, regardless of income, and those for which eligibility depends on financial need. The programs for which everyone is eligible—such as Social Security and unemployment insurance—are essentially insurance programs, the premiums for which are paid by payroll deductions and employer contributions. The need-based programs, which are supported by all taxpayers, are generally funded by the federal government but administered by the states.

Although the eligibility requirements for most government benefits are extremely stringent, vast numbers of people who are unquestionably eligible fail to take advantage of them simply because they don't know about their existence or about the application procedures. Since very few government agencies operate active outreach programs to inform prospective clients, the parent who needs help must be aggressive in finding out what is available. And, as we have noted earlier, false pride or a feeling of shame should not inhibit the efforts of a parent who has been abandoned, disabled, or indefinitely laid off.

Most readers of this book are unlikely to utilize the need-based programs because these are primarily intended to help people who spend most or all of their lives in poverty. But instability of employment or marriage has caused a number of solidly middle-class parents—typically mothers— to find themselves suddenly without income and threatened with foreclosure, eviction or the loss of essential services. For this reason, some understanding of the scope of need-based benefit programs can be useful.

Social Security Benefits

Although Social Security is generally seen as providing income for the retired, payments are also made before the retirement age to workers who are incapacitated and to the surviving spouse and dependent children of workers who have died. Benefits are payable regardless of need. In order to be eligible for payments, the worker must have paid Social Security taxes and earned "credits." Credits are earned at the rate of 4 per year, and most people need 40 credits (for 10 years of work) to qualify for benefits. Young people need fewer credits to qualify for disability or survivors' benefits.

The amount payable to the disabled worker or his survivors is based on what is called the *primary insurance amount,* or PIA, a figure that is determined by his average monthly earnings for a certain number of quarters. The surviving spouse of a covered worker is entitled to 100% of the worker's PIA at age 60 but can at any age opt for a parent's benefit (75% of the PIA) if he or she is caring for an eligible child under the age of 16.

The child of a retired, disabled, or deceased worker is entitled to benefits through the age of 18 (or 19 if in full-time attendance at a secondary school). If the child is disabled before age 22, however, eligibility continues without regard to age. The child's benefit is 50% of the PIA if the worker is retired or disabled, and 75% if the worker has died. If there are several children, each receives 50–75%, up to a maximum of 188% of the worker's PIA.

To be eligible for these benefits, children must meet the Social Security Administration's definitions of "dependent child." Under these criteria, all legitimate children are assumed eligible. Stepchildren are eligible if they lived with the insured worker for a certain length of time before the application is made or if the insured worker provided half the child's support. Legally adopted children are eligible but do not have to meet a dependency test unless they were adopted after the worker became eligible for benefits or by a surviving spouse after the worker's death. Illegitimate children may be eligible if they meet one of several alternative tests. Grandchildren and stepgrandchildren may, if they meet the dependency requirements, draw benefits on a grandparent's account provided that their parents were dead or disabled at the time that their grandparents became eligible for benefits.

Need-based Benefits

By far the most widespread assistance programs that benefit children directly have eligibility requirements based not only on the family's income but also on its structure. Thus, in order to be eligible, a child must live in a family with an income below the specified ceiling but also must be deprived of parental support through the death, disability, or absence of one parent.

Aid to Families with Dependent Children AFDC, available in all states, is jointly funded by the federal and state governments and administered by the states. Although the states must follow federal guidelines in determining eligibility, each state establishes its own standard of family need—that is, the income that a family requires to maintain a poverty-level standard of living. In addition, each state determines the percentage of this income that it will provide for. Some states pay 100%; others pay the difference between the needed income and the family's other income; others establish still lower levels of payment.

To meet the general eligibility requirements a family must not own more than $1,000 in resources, aside from its home, clothing, and furniture. In addition, the family's income (after deductions of up to $75 a month for work-related expenses and $160 per month per child for child-care costs) must not exceed the need standard established by the state.

A child living with adults to whom he is not related is not directly eligible for AFDC benefits but may be eligible for AFDC Foster Care payments, which are somewhat higher. To be eligible, the child must have been transferred from his home to a foster home or child-care institution by court order or voluntary agreement or placed under the care of the state or have received or been eligible for AFDC benefits during the month when he was removed from his home.

All able-bodied adult AFDC recipients with children over the age of five are required to register with the Work Incentive Program, an agency that provides job training and placement. If recipients fail to comply with the work requirements imposed by the program, they face the possibility of having their AFDC payments reduced or stopped altogether.

Food Stamp Program The federal Food Stamp Program, intended to provide nutrition for low-income individuals and families, is more liberal in its eligibility criteria than most other benefit programs, and hence it is open to families not eligible for AFDC. To be eligible, households must not own more than $2,000 in disposable assets ($3,000 if one member is age 60 or over) and have a gross income of not more than 130% and a net income of not more than 100% of the poverty guidelines set by the federal government.

Recipients receive a monthly allotment of coupons which they can redeem at supermarkets and other retail outlets for food of their choice (with certain exclusions). The value of the coupons is intended to provide the individual or family with an adequately nutritious diet at the poverty level and is periodically adjusted for fluctuations in the price of food.

School Lunch Programs The National School Lunch Program is federally funded to serve poor and near-poor schoolchildren, but participation is at the discretion of the individual school. Children whose family income is less than 130% of the amount set by federal guidelines receive lunches free; children of the near-poor (with family incomes between 130 and 185%) are charged a reduced price. In some areas the Summer Food Service Program provides the same benefit during the summer vacation. And in a limited number of low-income areas the School Breakfast Program supplements the benefits of the School Lunch Program.

Supplemental Security Income SSI, a federally funded program of cash assistance to those who are both needy and disabled, is also available to children. The child's disability must be a medically certified condition that can result in death or that will last for at least twelve months. The person must have resources of no more than $2,000 (up to $3,000 for a couple), excluding a house and household goods. Parental income must not exceed the SSI limits.

SSI benefits are generally higher than AFDC benefits and, unlike the latter, are adjusted for changes in the cost of living. In some states SSI eligibility qualifies the child automatically for Medicaid benefits.

State and Local General Assistance General assistance programs, which may be funded by states, counties, or local communities, typically provide emergency or stopgap assistance for cases not covered by AFDC. They may, for example, provide temporary help for a two-parent family that is ineligible for AFDC, a family that has applied for AFDC but has not yet received it, a family whose AFDC grant does not cover emergency needs (for back rent, for example, or the restoration of electric service that has been cut off because of nonpayment), or a pregnant teenager who needs assistance.

Eligibility criteria and benefit payments depend, of course, on the nature of the program. Maryland, for example, provides specified levels of payments for disabled persons, pregnant women with no other dependents, and other categories. New Hampshire's program, on the other hand, is intended to aid "whoever shall be poor and unable to support himself"—

a standard that has changed little since it was established in the seventeenth century.

Medical Benefits The federal Medicaid program provides neither direct medical service nor cash payments. Instead, it reimburses health-care providers who have indicated a willingness to accept Medicaid patients. All AFDC recipients are automatically eligible, but groups of medically needy people who do not meet AFDC criteria are also served.

State and county health departments generally operate prenatal, immunization, and well-baby clinics which render services free or for a nominal, income-adjusted fee.

Veterans' Benefits

Numerous pension and medical benefits are available to survivors of those who died and dependents of those who were disabled while serving in the armed services. Because the Department of Veterans Affairs is not noted for its responsiveness, information about eligibility and help in connection with the application procedure are probably more easily obtainable through one of the several veterans' organizations or through your local member of Congress.

Other Sources of Help

A number of other federal programs are intended to provide medical and nutritional support for mothers and children, but their funding and their current status are too uncertain to permit reliable description here. The staff of any local welfare office or other social service agency, however, can provide information on benefits, eligibility, and application procedures.

CHAPTER 9

HELPING YOUR ADULT CHILD

Although your legal obligation to support your child ends on the child's 18th birthday (except in the five states that specify 19 or 21 as the age of majority), this boundary line is likely to be meaningless in most stable families. At 18, your child will probably be less than halfway through a four-year college education and unable to finance it with the earnings from part-time jobs. In general, then, at least some continuing support is likely to be needed until college graduation at the earliest.

But often the child's need for financial help is likely to persist for several years after college graduation—or it may recur intermittently for the next couple of decades. To begin with, almost every career that merits the label "professional"—psychology, physics, or comparative literature, for example, as well as law and medicine—requires at least two and often as many as six years of postgraduate study. Medical schools and law schools, despite their very high tuition fees, provide almost nothing in the way of financial aid, and their curriculums leave little or no time for part-time work. The graduate programs in other professions do provide some support in the form of fellowships, grants, and assistantships, but these can't be relied on, since they come and go with changes in government policy or university budget. In any event, they are rarely adequate to cover all costs, and they may not be available until your child has proved herself by a year of good work at her own expense.

There are other circumstances in which you may find yourself subsidizing your child: contributing to or providing the down payment on his first house, for example, or helping to capitalize a child's business venture or professional practice, or helping your child indirectly by paying for some of your grandchildren's "extras," such as summer camp, ballet or music lessons, or a trip abroad.

All of these expenditures are likely to be "happy" ones, because they presumably help further the child's career or offer him relief from financial stress at a particularly difficult time. But you may also confront some less happy situations: a retarded or disabled child's need for lifetime support and care (see Chapter 11); a child's (and her children's) need for financial help in the aftermath of a marriage break-up; a long or chronic illness, mental or physical, that interferes with the child's employment in addition to piling up medical bills; support for an out-of-wedlock grandchild; or even legal fees to extricate your child from criminal charges or bankruptcy.

Some of these unhappy situations can, of course, have happy endings. The child's financial emergency passes and you are left with the satisfaction of having made it less stressful than it might have been. But there is also the possibility that a "happy" kind of support can turn unhappy. What happens, for example, if your daughter and her husband divorce only a year after you have provided the down payment on their house or given them a lump sum with which to start or buy a business?

Whether the circumstances are happy or unhappy, the need for financial assistance often arises suddenly and is likely to be met impulsively (by the parent who has the assets to spare) or under severe stress (by the parent who doesn't); the help may be offered generously and with pleasure or grudgingly with grave misgivings. In either circumstance, it is all too often given without consideration of the following questions:

- What are the tax implications for the donor and the recipient?
- How will the gift or loan affect the relationship between the donor and the recipient?
- Will a gift to one child provoke resentment from his siblings—toward him, toward you, or toward both of you?
- If your aid takes the form of a loan, what do you plan to do if it is not repaid?
- How will a gift (or a loan that is not repaid) affect your present financial security or your retirement plans?

These questions indicate that there are better and worse ways of helping your adult child. And some forms of help, which are just as effective as others, not only have tax consequences that can lower a gift's actual costs but also reduce the risk of friction and stress within the family.

WHERE WILL THE MONEY COME FROM?

When a child's need for a substantial amount of financial help arises, your first step is to choose the source of funds that can serve the purpose most effectively. If your help is to take the form of a gift, you will want to give assets that are least costly to you in terms of your loss of their yield or most burdensome in terms of their tax liability. Thus, for example, it may be better for you to liquidate fully taxable securities rather than tax-exempt municipal bonds, or to give cash which is earning low interest rather than liquidate securities that produce a high yield or have good prospects for appreciation, or to give appreciated property so that the gain on a later sale is taxed at your child's presumably lower rate rather than yours. If helping your child requires you to take out a loan or to cosign a loan for him, you need to choose a loan that is least costly to you in interest charges and least threatening to your own credit status and to your net worth should the loan lapse into default.

If you plan to borrow the money yourself, consider the following sources:

- If you have a "whole life" insurance policy, you may be able to borrow its cash value at a rate of interest significantly lower than what a commercial lender would charge. If you have difficulty in repaying it, the worst that can happen is that the face value of the policy will be reduced by the amount of the loan.
- If you have a certificate of deposit or a passbook savings account that you are willing to use as collateral, most banks will offer you a discount on their conventional loan interest.
- If you have a portfolio of securities that can serve as collateral, most stockbrokers will lend you money against it at rates that may be competitive with bank rates. If the stock market is at a low ebb, such a loan may be preferable to liquidating your securities at low prices.
- Because only the interest on home mortgages is fully tax-deductible, most lending institutions offer "home equity" loans. These may be an attractive source of funds provided you have looked carefully at the various closing costs that are not included in the advertised interest rates.

If you cosign a loan or a mortgage with your child, bear in mind that you will be responsible for the entire debt balance should the child default and that listing this obligation on future credit applications may result in your being disapproved for further credit—such as a new-car loan.

OUTRIGHT GIFTS

Whether it takes the form of cash, securities, real estate, or other assets, an outright gift with no strings attached is often the best form of help. It implies not only your love and support but also your confidence that the child will use the assets maturely and appropriately. Moreover, if you give during your lifetime assets that you would otherwise leave to your child after your death, you gain the opportunity to enjoy the child's gratitude and to witness the uses to which the gift is put. In addition, your child is likely to need and value your gift far more if she gets it when she is in her twenties or thirties than she would if she inherits it through your will when she is in her fifties.

Gifts and Taxes

Gifts in any amount are tax-exempt for the recipient, although she will, of course, be liable for income tax on their yield or growth after she takes possession of them. But your gifts to the same individual totaling more than $10,000 ($20,000 if made with the consent of your spouse) in a single calendar year are subject to the Federal Gift and Estate Tax—a tax for which the *donor* is liable.

Because this $10,000/$20,000 exemption generally exceeds the amount that most middle-income parents are likely to give to one child in a single year and because, as we shall see, there are several ways of exceeding this limit without incurring tax liability, the "gift" tax aspects of the federal gift and estate tax are likely to concern only the very rich. The "estate" aspects of the tax may well be of interest to you, but because they relate to estate planning, we shall deal with them in Chapter 11.

Gifts of the size that most parents make are likely to be tax-exempt. If you are planning to help your child with a very substantial sum—say, the down payment on a house, or funds to capitalize a new business venture—you would probably be wiser to offer the help by means of a loan. But even if your help takes the form of an outright gift, there are several perfectly legal strategies by which you can avoid liability for gift tax.

If, for example, you and your spouse want to give $40,000 to a daughter, you can avoid gift-tax liability by giving her $20,000 on December 31 and another $20,000 the next day, which is the start of a new calendar year. And you can give $20,000 to her and another $20,000 simultaneously to her spouse or child who, in turn, can give it to or use it for her. Or you and your spouse can deposit any amount in a bank, money market, or brokerage account registered in joint tenancy with your daughter and instruct her to withdraw it in increments amounting to less than $20,000 per calendar year, since no "gift" takes effect until she actually withdraws money from the account. Unless her withdrawals exceed the $10,000/$20,000 limit in a single year, no gift tax is incurred. Under this arrangement, however, you remain liable for the tax on its yield as long as you control the account.

If you can afford to part with $100,000 immediately, you can avoid the gift tax by lending this sum to your child and subsequently forgiving the annual repayments of $10,000/$20,000 as each falls due.

Giving Cash, Securities, and Other Assets

Cash gifts of any significant size should, of course, be made by check so that a written record remains in case the IRS should audit either you or the recipient. A canceled check is also useful to settle disputes among your children if you give one child a large gift with the understanding that the amount will be deducted from his share of his inheritance.

Gifts need not, of course, take the form of cash. If, for example, you give your child income-producing real estate, the income it yields will be taxed at his rate rather than yours. Giving away securities that have appreciated substantially can offer you some tax advantage. Suppose, for example, you own shares that cost you $20 per share and are now worth $45. If you sell them in order to raise cash for your child, you will pay income tax on your $25-per-share profit. But if you were to give the shares to your child, he will, when he sells them, pay tax on the same $25-per-share profit (because the recipient of a gift assumes the donor's "cost basis") but within his tax bracket, which is presumably lower than yours. And if he does not sell them, the dividends may be taxed more lightly. On the other hand, if you were to retain them in your own name and pass them on to him through your will, his "stepped up" cost basis will be the value of the shares at the time of your death, and if he sells them at this price, he would pay no tax at all.

The procedures for giving a child either securities or real estate are simple. If the securities are registered in your own name, simply endorse them and mail them to the issuing corporation for reissue in the child's name. If they are held in a broker's "street account," you need merely instruct the broker to open an account in your child's name and transfer to it the securities you intend to give her. She can, of course, withdraw them from the account or sell them as soon as the transfer has been completed. In the case of real estate, you must sign and deliver to the child a new deed, which should be recorded in the office of the local register of deeds.

Problems with Gifts

Although the procedure itself is simple enough, giving your child a gift "with no strings attached" can have complex ramifications. On the one hand, if the gift is misused—if the child drops out of college after you have paid his tuition, or if the business that your gift has capitalized fails—recriminations are very difficult to avoid. On the other hand, if all goes as planned, the recipient's siblings may feel that they have not been treated fairly, even though their needs may have been very different. For these reasons, many parents feel that the preferable way of providing financial support to a child is through a loan.

LOANS

Even though it need not involve interest, and even though its repayment can be postponed indefinitely or even "forgiven," a loan would appear to have a number of advantages over a no-strings-attached gift. Not only does it avoid sibling jealousy but, no matter how lenient its terms, its businesslike tone can reinforce the child's responsibility to use the money wisely and to repay it when it becomes due. At the same time, it can spare the child the delays and embarrassment of a bank credit check and provide him with cash either at no interest or at a rate lower than any lending institution would charge. The parent can also benefit from this arrangement if he charges an interest rate that is somewhat higher than the current yield on some of his own investments.

Some Risks

On the other hand, the family loan is not without its problems. Even though it is a more "businesslike" arrangement than a gift and obligates the borrower eventually to repay the money to the parents, the borrower's siblings may be jealous or resentful over what they see as favoritism. And even though the lending parent intends to regard the loan as a business arrangement, it may be difficult for him to avoid an intrusive monitoring of the borrower's use of the money or recriminations if the money should be squandered.

This temptation of the lender to supervise or participate in the borrower's decisions or to offer unwelcome advice is likely to become especially troublesome if the loan is a substantial one intended for a business venture. In such circumstances the parent might be wiser not to lend the money but to use it to buy either a partnership interest or shares of stock in the child's business venture and thus acquire the right to supervise or influence the venture's policies. Of course, this strategy is no panacea. The lender's advice and guidance may be inappropriate as well as unwelcome, and the borrower may resent having to part permanently with a share of the business for the sake of initial financing.

The problem of lender involvement also makes its appearance when the loan is intended to provide part or all of the down payment on a child's house. In such cases it may be very difficult for the lender to restrain himself from offering advice on the basis of his "greater experience." Although this experience may have some validity, much of it is likely to be irrelevant in terms of the current market and generational differences in tastes and lifestyle preferences.

Documenting the Loan

Any loan more substantial than a short-term, "tide me over" sum of a few hundred dollars should be documented by a promissory note, a form available at stationery or office-supply stores. The note should specify either that the loan is repayable on or by a certain date or, alternatively, at any time that the lender demands repayment. It should also specify the payment schedule and the rate of interest, if any. And, of course, it should be dated, signed by the borrower, and retained by the lender until it has been paid in full.

If the loan is substantial, it should be "secured"; that is, the borrower should provide some sort of collateral—a first or second mortgage on real estate, for example, or a lien on a motor vehicle or any other asset with value equivalent to that of the loan—that the lender can foreclose on or take possession of should the borrower default on the loan. But in the event of default, the lender must be willing to take his child to court in order to collect—a process that many parents are reluctant to undertake. Nevertheless, securing the loan is important because, if the borrower declares bankruptcy, secured debts are given priority over unsecured debts. And if the borrower is subsequently divorced, the collateral remains as security for repayment of the loan.

Loans and Taxes

Although the payment of interest makes any parent-child loan more businesslike, its effect on the tax situation of both lender and borrower needs to be considered carefully. Because the Tax Reform Act of 1986 phased out the tax-deductibility of interest payments on all loans other than home mortgages, the borrower gets little or no tax advantage, and hence interest makes the loan more costly to him. The lender, on the other hand, must pay income tax on the interest he receives, and this reduces his yield below what he might get from a tax-free municipal bond.

Interest-free loans—which the IRS calls "gift loans"—usually have no income-tax consequences unless they are substantial. The IRS has ruled that an interest-free loan includes *as a gift from the lender to the borrower* the interest that the lender would normally have collected at the prevailing rate. But to generate an annual interest of more than $10,000/$20,000 (the maximum exemption under the Federal Gift and Estate Tax) the principal would have to be very much larger than what most parents could or would lend a child. Special rules apply to loans with below-market interest rates which may result in taxable income being attributed to the buyer. (These are explained in IRS Publication 550.)

Although lenders are allowed an income-tax deduction for "bad debts," the IRS scrutinizes rather closely defaults in which the borrower is a child or other close relative of the lender. If your child defaults on a loan, you must, before tax- deducting it as a bad debt, be prepared to document the loan and to demonstrate that you took legal steps to enforce its collection.

Cosigning a Child's Loan

If you have no assets to give or lend a child who wants to buy a home or a car, launch a new business venture, or buy into an existing one, you might offer to act as cosigner on a bank loan that he applies for. Your cosigning means, of course, that, although he will be expected to make all repayments on schedule, you assume complete responsibility for the entire balance if he should default.

Cosigning the child's loan offers the advantage of eliminating a cash outlay on your part, but it may also give you a false sense of security if you assume that the bank's loan officer will scrutinize your child's business plans and reject the loan if they strike him as harebrained. Contrary to their advertising, banks do not make loans to borrowers with brilliant ideas but no collateral. They are interested only in the probability of getting their money back while earning interest in the meantime. Hence, your cosigning will probably help get the loan approved, but the approval does not in any way signify that your child's plans are viable.

SPECIAL SITUATIONS

College Costs

Because room and board costs in college dorms and dining halls are usually higher than they are in the surrounding community, many students save money and enjoy a higher standard of living by renting a house or apartment and cooking for themselves.

Some parents have made this arrangement even more economical by buying a house or condominium close to campus and renting it to their child (and perhaps two or three classmates) for a reasonable monthly payment. This rental income allows the parent all the depreciation and other tax deductions available for income-producing real estate and, because the price of property in college communities tends to remain stable or to rise over the years, such an investment may be a good one, especially if more than one of your children are likely to attend the same college or if your child remains on the campus for two or three additional years for graduate study.

Of course, there are risks and hazards. Your child may drop out of school. Student tenants are notoriously destructive and may fail to pay their share of the rent. Property close to campus is readily marketable, but marketability may drop off rapidly as distance from the campus increases. Property taxes tend to be high in college communities. Nevertheless, if you investigate this possibility carefully, you may find it rewarding.

Helping Your Child Buy a Home

Given the cost of an average house and the average income of a young couple, parental help with the down payment seems almost essential. But because a request for this kind of help is probably the most substantial you'll ever get, you need to consider very carefully your available alternatives and their potential consequences.

Buying the house yourself on a cash-plus-mortgage basis and renting it to your child may have the same tax and investment advantages described on the preceding page, and it may permit him eventually to repay your investment or buy you out and leave you with some profit. But, in addition to tying up both your capital and your credit, it presents other problems. You and your child may disagree on the style, price, or location of the house, and you, of course, should have the last word since the investment is entirely yours. Your child's job may require a move shortly after the purchase. Your child's marriage may fall apart, or your child may be unable to pay the rent or to maintain the property in decent condition. Of course, many of these problems can arise even if you make the down payment in the form of a gift, but in such circumstances you are not left holding a piece of property that ties up your capital and requires tax payments and other out-of-pocket disbursements until you can get it off your hands.

An alternative that is preferable in some respects is called *equity sharing*. Under this plan, the parents contribute part or all of the down payment in return for part ownership in the property. The arrangement can be rather flexible. If, for example, the child pays the parent a monthly rental in addition to meeting his share of the mortgage payments, the parent can enjoy all the tax advantages of income-producing real estate and the child can tax-deduct the interest on his share of the mortgage payments. Insurance premiums, property taxes, and similar expenses are shared by parent and child in proportion to their equity, though routine maintenance is usually the child's responsibility. If the child's income increases, he can buy the parent's share at an agreed-upon price or, if the house is sold, parent and child share the proceeds in proportion to their equity.

Compared to an outright gift or parent ownership of the child's house, equity sharing presumably gives the child a far greater sense of responsibility for maintaining the property and meeting its costs. But some problems remain. There must be mutual agreement on the price, location, style, and condition of the house under consideration. If parent and child each hold a 50% equity interest, they may reach a deadlock on important decisions about maintaining, improving, or selling the property. And if your child's spouse participates in the arrangement and subsequently divorces, you may find yourself in partnership with your child's "ex."

A NOTE OF CAUTION

Thus far we have dealt with the various alternatives you have for helping your child. But there is one further alternative that needs emphasis: your right to say "no." No matter how legitimate your child's request for help, once he is an adult your first obligation is to your spouse, any minor children, and yourself. If helping your child seriously jeopardizes your current standard of living or your own security in retirement or old age, you will be doing the child no favor, because you may well become dependent on him in later years. Like other luxuries, helping a child is fine if you can afford it but foolhardy if you can't.

C H A P T E R   1 0

THE SEVERELY
HANDICAPPED CHILD

Although rehabilitation services often achieve remark-able results in making both physically and mentally handicapped persons productive and self-sufficient, and although the handicapped face far less social rejection and job discrimination than they once did, parents of severely handicapped children face problems that can drain them both emotionally and economically. Through much of their lifetimes, they may struggle with the question of whether to institutionalize the child or keep him at home. And, whatever their decision, the costs of rehabilitation, custodial, medical, and educational services can devastate their standard of living. But adding to this burden is their constant concern about "what will happen when we're no longer here to take care of him."

Such parents can lighten their burden by learning as much as possible about the various sources of support and assistance, both private and public, that are available to their child. But many of them fail to do this—not because of apathy or incompetence but because they feel that asking for help is somehow shameful, that families should be able to solve their own problems, and that using a "social agency" places them in the position of the widely (though unfairly) stigmatized "bums on welfare." This feeling of shame, and their insistence on "paying their own way," can condemn such parents to a lifetime of near-poverty even though they are eligible for various forms of supportive services and financial help.

But it is also possible to regard both the public and private agencies that serve the handicapped as similar to insurance companies. Just as we pay premiums to protect ourselves against losses due to death or disability, so too we pay taxes (or make charitable contributions) to support agencies that help protect parents from the catastrophic costs of a handicapped child. And just as we feel no shame whatever in filing an insurance claim after an accident—because, after all, we have been paying premiums for years—so we need feel no stigma whatever in utilizing the agencies which, after all, we have been supporting through taxes and contributions. Like the insurance companies, they are "in business" for the sole purpose of protecting us against misfortune.

Parents who adopt this more objective and more rational view are likely to discover that there are many sources of financial support and that they do not have to be destitute to qualify their child for valuable help.

PRIVATE AGENCIES

There is virtually no severely handicapping condition—mental retardation, cerebral palsy, schizophrenia, spina bifida, kidney disease, paraplegia—that does not have some sort of voluntary organization devoted to finding its cure and to providing its victims and their families with assistance in various forms. Some of these organizations are little more than parent support groups, but many of them have become large and powerful national institutions that have lobbied successfully, at both the state and the federal levels, for public rehabilitation and custodial services as well as research funds. As a result of their efforts, to cite only two examples, a variety of cost-free services are available to the blind, regardless of income, and so is kidney dialysis—a procedure that would be unbearably expensive for any but the wealthiest families.

Active contact with one of these private organizations can, at the very least, bring parents in touch with other parents who have suffered similar misfortune, and such meetings can provide not only emotional support but also practical advice on coping with specific problems, large and small.

Perhaps more important, these agencies can inform parents about the various sources of private and public support, their eligibility requirements, and the procedures for filing an application for assistance.

SOURCES OF PUBLIC SUPPORT

State and Local Services

The number and quality of state and local services are so heavily dependent on the social and economic climate of the state and on its current budgetary situation that almost any generalization is meaningless. Many states provide both rehabilitative and custodial services on a fee-for-service basis, with fees adjusted to the family's income and no fee charged for the indigent. For this reason, parents who are not wealthy and who anticipate that their child will require long-term or lifetime support or custodial care may want to take steps to ensure that he will be "indigent" as soon as he reaches majority (see p. 183).

Medicare

Although Medicare is widely regarded as designed primarily for the benefit of the elderly, disabled people under the age of 65 who have been receiving Social Security disability benefits for two years or more may be able to have some of their medical costs met through this program—again without regard to the family's income.

Medicaid

Medicaid is a health-care program with eligibility requirements similar to those for SSI. Like SSI, it will be available to the disabled child only after he reaches the age of majority unless his parents themselves qualify.

Family Benefits

If you are eligible for retirement or disability benefits, other members of your family may receive benefits as well. Your spouse will receive benefits if he or she is at least 62 years old or is under 62 but is caring for a child under age 16. Your children will receive benefits if they are under 18 and unmarried, or under 19 but still in school, or 18 or older but disabled. If you are divorced, your ex-spouse may be eligible for benefits.

Social Security Survivors Benefits

If you earned enough Social Security credits during your lifetime, your surviving family members may be eligible for benefits. These members include a widow or widower age 60 or older, 50 or older if disabled, and of any age if caring for a child under the age of 16. Your children are entitled to benefits if they are under 18 and unmarried, or under 19 but still in school, or 18 or older but disabled. Your parents may receive benefits if you were their primary means of support. A special one-time payment of $225 may be made to your surviving spouse or minor children, and your ex-spouse may be eligible for a widow or widower's benefits.

Supplemental Security Income

Supplemental Security Income (SSI) is a means-based assistance program intended to supplement the incomes of the very poor. Unless his parents are poor, a disabled child is likely to be ineligible (because his income is considered to be that of his parents) but he may become eligible as soon as he attains majority, since at that time his parents are no longer responsible for his support. Because the means test is quite strict, parents can jeopardize their child's future eligibility by transferring assets to him during their lifetimes or after their deaths, regardless of whether these assets are held in the child's name or in a custodial, guardian, or trust account.

PLANNING AHEAD FOR THE DISABLED CHILD

Guardianship

Until the child reaches the age of majority, his parents are his legal guardians and generally have the right to manage any inheritances or other assets that he receives. But this guardianship ends as soon as the child becomes an adult unless the child is legally declared incompetent. If, then, the child is severely retarded or otherwise unable to manage his own assets, parents should apply to the probate court for a formal determination of the child's incompetence and for their appointment as guardians. In addition, their wills should nominate a guardian who will succeed them upon the death of the surviving parent. If the disability is likely to be permanent, the guardian should preferably be young as well as trustworthy, although he or she in turn, may ask the court to name or approve his successor.

Leaving Your Child Indigent

Very wealthy parents are likely to be undaunted by the prospect that the child's custodial care will have to continue long after their deaths. They need merely bequeath assets to a trust established for the child in an amount sufficient to pay for the indefinite continuation of the same private support or custodial care that the child received while they were alive.

Parents with moderate incomes face a totally different situation. They will be forced to leave their child dependent to some degree on government benefits because they are almost certainly unable to pay for his care for a period of perhaps thirty years after their own deaths. One strategy is to leave the child assets that will pay for a few years of care and then allow him to become a public charge, since public institutions charge no fees to the indigent other than what the indigent receives from public entitlement programs. An alternative strategy is to make certain that the child is, in fact, indigent at the time the parents die, thus ensuring their child's initial entitlement to government benefits.

At first glance, the prospect of making your disabled child indigent may seem cruel and unjust. But, since professionally managed public institutions make little or no distinction in their treatment of paying and nonpaying residents, you are doing the child no harm. On the other hand, whatever assets you leave for the care of the child will be quickly absorbed by the maintenance expenses and will reduce the inheritance that his siblings might receive.

If you adopt this approach, you should instruct grandparents or other relatives who have designated him as a beneficiary to revise their wills so as to disinherit him and to remove him as a beneficiary of their life insurance policies. Of course, you, too, should explicitly disinherit him in your own will, since any assets bequeathed to him (or in care of his guardian or trustee) may be claimed by a public institution to pay for his care and will probably disqualify him from any means-based form of public assistance.

If you are concerned about furnishing your child with some comforts that are unlikely to be provided by government benefits or by the generally austere public institutions, you can do this in two ways without disqualifying him from public assistance.

Bequest to a Sibling If you leave a fund to a sibling or other relative of the disabled child, or to a family friend, with the suggestion that it be used only to provide "extras" and comforts for your child, you will not jeopardize the disabled person's indigency status, because the person to whom you leave the money has no *legal* obligation to use the gift for the benefit of the disabled person.

This arrangement, simple and informal though it is, is not without problems. To begin with, the recipient of the funds is under no legal obligation to use them for the benefit of the disabled person, and he may be tempted to divert them to his own use or that of another. Even if he recognizes and honors his moral obligation, he must pay income tax on their yield. In addition, the money, because it is in his own name, is vulnerable to the claims of his creditors or may be dissipated in a business reversal or a divorce. On the other hand, if the bequest proves insufficient, the recipient may feel obligated to supplement it with his own money. Lastly, if he should die before your disabled child, the money may go to someone who does not recognize or does not respect its original purpose.

The "Luxury" Trust Parents who plan to leave a substantial amount of money for the benefit of their disabled child should consider using either a testamentary trust (see p. 189). or a living trust (see p. 192). One advantage of such a trust is that the child cannot outlive it, since a series of successor trustees can be appointed to serve as long as there are assets in the trust. In the case of a disabled child, however, the trust must be worded very carefully in order to maintain the disabled person's eligibility for means-based benefits and to prevent a custodial institution from making claims against it for past and future services.

Most conventional trusts specify that the trustee is to distribute income and/or principal to the beneficiaries either entirely at his own discretion or within clearly prescribed limits or for carefully specified purposes. If the beneficiary is a disabled person, however, giving the trustee complete discretion or specifying that the trustee must use trust assets for the beneficiary's "maintenance" or "support" is likely to jeopardize the disabled person's indigency status, render him ineligible for means-based government benefits, and expose the trust assets to claims by a custodial institution.

To prevent the trust assets from being regarded as a resource of the disabled person and to keep them immune from state claims for reimbursement, the trust must be drafted so as to deny either the beneficiary or the trustee the right to use trust funds to provide food, shelter, or clothing for the disabled person. The purposes of the trust might, for example, be specified as: (1) to provide the disabled child with a quality of life higher than that provided by public entitlement programs, and (2) to provide the child with an appropriate funeral and burial.

The trustee should be given absolute power to accumulate income and complete discretion as to whether interest, principal, or both are to be distributed. But such discretion should be restricted by a clause specifying that the trustee is not to use trust funds for the purpose of providing the beneficiary with food, clothing, or shelter or, alternatively, that the funds may be used only to meet the disabled child's needs beyond those met by public assistance and support.

This type of trust has, for obvious reasons, been called a "luxury trust." But this should not imply that it is usable only by wealthy parents. The fact that its funds can be used only for limited purposes means that a relatively small amount of money, properly invested, can last a long time and go a long way in improving the quality of life for a disabled child.

Whatever the strategy, planning for a disabled child should always be done with the help of a lawyer skilled in estate planning.

CHAPTER 11

ESTATE PLANNING TO
PROTECT YOUR CHILDREN

We dealt with wills and estate planning in a deliberately simple fashion in Chapter 3, because at that point we assumed that your assets were few and your children were young, and that your will's primary function was to designate a guardian for your minor children. In this chapter we assume that your circumstances have changed: your assets have increased, your children are nearing adulthood, and the death rate for your age group is slowly rising. And so your concern about your estate plan now centers on its function in transferring your assets to your survivors after your death. We shall deal, then, with the will as a transfer vehicle and with some other methods of transfer that you may find more suitable.

TRANSFERRING ASSETS THROUGH A WILL

If you haven't bothered to draft a will—or to update a twenty-year-old version—you are doing no harm to yourself, but you may inflict substantial damage on your survivors. At best, their memories of you may be tarnished by "the mess he left us" as they try to create order out of a chaos of unassorted and unbequeathed assets. At worst, in absence of a properly drawn will, along with other estate-planning strategies, your assets may pass into the hands of people you would not have chosen as beneficiaries, or they may be needlessly eroded by probate costs and death taxes, or they may not become available to your survivors for months or even years after your death.

If you die without a will, your probate assets will be distributed by your local probate court to those people whom the state recognizes as your "heirs at law." Although state laws differ in minor details, this usually means that your spouse will receive one-third to one-half of your probate estate, and your children, regardless of age, will get the rest, even though you would have preferred to leave everything to your spouse and let her pass the residue to the children upon her death. It may mean, also, that nothing passes to children of your first marriage, to friends, or to a favorite charity or activist organization. And, even if your probate estate is of only moderate size, it means that the court will appoint a personal representative (perhaps the judge's favorite bank or political crony) to liquidate and distribute your assets and that the bonding premiums and the personal representative's fees will be charged against your estate.

All of this can be avoided by means of a properly drawn will. Because it can specify precisely who is to receive what proportion of your estate, you can leave assets to children of a former marriage, to friends, and to others who may not be your "heirs at law," although a will cannot entirely disinherit a surviving spouse. You can designate as your personal representative a friend or relative and specify that he serve without bonding. You can avoid or reduce any federal estate tax (see p. 193) that might be chargeable against your estate.

Choosing Your Beneficiaries

Normally, husbands and wives each make a will leaving all assets to each other, with the children as beneficiaries after the deaths of both. Single parents of adult children generally leave everything to the children. You can, of course, amend your will periodically to reflect changes in your family. Your original will, for example, might have left assets to your children in equal shares. But if one of your children becomes rich and another is facing all sorts of financial problems, there is no reason why you should not leave a larger share to the one who needs it more. In short, a will allows you to decide who deserves and who can best use your assets after your death, or whom you intend to disinherit entirely.

But a simple will gives you little or no control over *how* your assets will be used, because it generally transfers them to your beneficiaries with no long-term conditions as to their use. In general, they are free to spend it for whatever purpose and at whatever rate they choose. This may give you pause if, for example, your spouse is completely inexperienced in managing money, or if your children, even though they have reached adulthood, are immature or have spendthrift tendencies. In these circumstances, many parents supplement their wills with a testamentary trust.

The Testamentary Trust

A testamentary trust is a trust created within your will. Under this arrangement, the trust, managed by a trustee whom you designate, becomes the sole beneficiary of everything you leave through your will. And the trust's terms can specify virtually any conditions you want to impose on the use of your assets after your death.

If, for example, your children seem immature, you can direct the trustee to withhold all of their inheritance until they reach the age of 25 or 30, or to make limited payments to them over a period of several years. Or if you suspect that your son is a bit lazy, you can motivate him by specifying that the trust will pay him annually only an amount equal to what he earns. And if you feel that your spouse is incapable of managing her inheritance prudently, your trust can specify a professional trustee to manage the assets and make periodic payments to your spouse from principal or yield at whatever rate and on whatever schedule you prefer.

Establishing a testamentary trust costs little when it's done in connection with a will and it provides you with a good measure of reassurance that whatever probate assets you leave will not be dissipated by your survivors. But a testamentary trust has one serious limitation: because it is a receptacle for your probate assets transferred by will, your will must undergo probate administration before your assets can pass to the trust.

THE PROBLEM OF PROBATE

Of course, lack of control over how your assets will be used may not concern you unduly. A far more widespread problem—and one that is likely to affect you if your probate assets amount to more than a few thousand dollars—is the probate court process. Whether or not you have a will, administration of your estate by the probate court is inevitable if you leave assets that are in your name alone—unless you take steps to avoid it.

The probating of an estate is society's way of ensuring, through supervision by the county probate court, that after your death your debts and taxes are paid and the residue is properly distributed among the appropriate survivors—those named in your will or, if you left no will, your "heirs at law." If you leave any assets that are titled in your name alone—a bank account, for example, or securities, or real estate—those are considered "probate" assets, which cannot pass to your survivors without administration by the probate court. Although most states have adopted "small estate" transfer procedures that eliminate the delays of full probate, these are severely limited: they generally cannot be used if the assets include real estate or if their value exceeds a relatively small amount.

Although the principles behind probate are fair enough, the process itself is usually slow, expensive, and thoroughly exasperating, sometimes tying up the survivors' inheritances for years while the personal representative, under supervision by the probate court, carries out the lengthy legal process of settling your estate. In addition, because probate is a public process, any interested person can find out the value of your probate estate, the identities of your beneficiaries, and any conditions you place on their bequests. For all these reasons many authorities on estate planning make as their first priority the avoidance of probate.

Joint Ownership

Because "probate assets" consist only of those owned by *you alone*, one way to avoid probate is to place most or all of your assets in joint ownership with a spouse, a cohabitant, or an adult child. Joint ownership has been called "the poor man's will" because on the death of one of the joint "tenants" ownership of the entire property passes automatically to the survivor without the need for probate administration.*
Hence, one way of "willing" an asset to your children is to place it in joint ownership between you and them. Joint ownership also is useful for unmarried cohabitants to protect one another financially because, if one of them dies without a will, the survivor is not recognized as an "heir at law," and will inherit nothing. And, even if there is a will, the surviving cohabitant will enjoy none of the concessions and advantages that the law provides for legal spouses.

Joint ownership can be used for almost any kind of property—from household furnishings, jewelry, or a coin collection to a house, a bank account, a mutual fund, or a securities portfolio—and it can involve any number of owners: for example, spouses and their two children, or grandparents and grandchildren. Moreover, it's simple to establish at little

---

*Joint ownership, often called "joint tenancy," implies "rights of survivorship" and is often abbreviated on bank accounts and stock certificates as "JTWROS."

or no cost. For a bank or brokerage account, it requires nothing more than the signing of new signature cards or registration documents. For real estate, a new deed can be prepared and recorded at minimal cost. For coin collections, furniture, jewelry, and other tangible property, a written statement acknowledging joint ownership is sufficient.

But joint ownership can, in some cases, be hazardous to your wealth. For one thing, once established, it may be impossible to unwind without the consent of all joint owners. Hence, once you register assets in joint tenancy, you can no longer will them to a different beneficiary. Worse yet, the joint ownership may survive desertion, alienation between tenants, and other unforeseeable changes in the relationship of the joint tenants. And so, because either tenant is entitled to the jointly held assets, joint ownership must never be used if their relationship is, or may some day become, unstable. If it is, there is the danger that one joint-tenant spouse or cohabitant may decamp suddenly with the assets and a new partner. In addition, jointly held assets are vulnerable to either tenant's creditors. Thus, if your joint-tenant son goes bankrupt, part of your jointly held assets will be vulnerable to the claims of his creditors.

Perhaps the greatest hazard of joint ownership stems from the fact that there is no way of predicting which of the tenants will be the first to die or which will survive the others. Suppose, for example, that you die having held your securities jointly with your son and daughter. They would remain as the surviving joint owners, but if your son should die either before your death or shortly thereafter, your daughter would own it all and be under no obligation to share it with your son's children. At best joint ownership is a short-term solution, because on the death of the other tenant or tenants the property belongs solely to the survivor—and hence will be probatable unless he or she takes steps to avoid probate.

Joint ownership does not, of course, obviate the need for a will, because it cannot provide for inheritance if both tenants die simultaneously. In addition, a will is necessary not only to designate a guardian for your minor children but also to dispose of assets that could not be placed into joint ownership (proceeds of a wrongful death claim, for example) or that you neglected to transfer into joint ownership.

Despite these hazards and limitations, however, joint ownership can, for stable families, serve as an extremely effective device for probate-avoidance. If spouses can place virtually everything they own into joint ownership, each of them may, on their death, leave so little solely owned property that it qualifies for their state's "small estate" transfer procedure and avoids the full-fledged probate process.

The Revocable Living Trust

A far more effective probate-avoidance device—and one that eliminates not only the hazards of joint ownership but also the risk of inheritance by financially naive or immature survivors—is a living trust. Because so many third-rate novels and soap operas contain characters who live on "a trust my grandfather left me," many people below the millionaire level conclude that a trust is an arcane device that helps the very rich to evade taxes or control their black-sheep children—and certainly not something that they themselves could use to advantage. And the fact that the concept of a trust is not easy to grasp reinforces their indifference or skepticism. Nevertheless, once you understand its advantages, you may feel, as increasing numbers of the nonrich do, that a trust would be a valuable supplement to your will.

Although trusts come in a multiplicity of shapes and sizes, the type most commonly used to avoid probate is the revocable living, or *inter vivos*, trust. Such a trust is similar in some respects to a corporation: although it is not a human being, it can own property of any kind, and its property is under the control of one or more trustees, whose functions are similar to those of a corporation's executive officer. And like a corporation's by-laws, the trust document spells out very clearly the powers of the trustee(s) as well as how, when, for whom, and for what purposes he, she, or it may disburse the trust assets.

Having established "The John L. Smith Trust" and transferred all or most of your assets into it, you can, during your lifetime, act as your own trustee or as co-trustee with your spouse or, if you want your assets managed professionally, you can designate a bank or trust company as trustee. The trust document will also designate one or more successor trustees because, as we shall see, one of the advantages of a trust is that it is intended to outlive you or to function if you become disabled.

During your lifetime, you can, as trustee, buy, sell, use, spend, or give away the trust assets, or move assets into or out of trust ownership, just as you would do with your own property. And, of course, you will pay taxes on any income the trust receives. But on the instant of your death, all trust assets belong to the trust and not to you. Hence they need not be probated and they are not generally subject to the claims of your personal creditors.

But probate-avoidance is only one advantage of the trust. It offers you, in addition, all the protection provided by the testamentary trust against possible misuse of your money by your survivors (see p. 189). A trust is especially useful if you are a homeowner or if you own a business of any kind. If you have only a will, the probate process can hold up the sale of your home or bring your business to a complete halt for months, sometimes years, until your probate estate has been settled. But if your home or business is owned by your trust, it passes to your survivors without probate administration. Your home can be sold immediately, and your business can continue without interruption, managed by the trustee or by someone you have authorized him to employ.

Prior to your death, you can amend or revoke your trust at any time your circumstances change. But a trust does not eliminate the need for a will. For one thing, a trust cannot legally designate a guardian for your minor children. For another, it cannot dispose of property that it doesn't own—property that, despite your best efforts, you may have neglected to transfer into the trust prior to your death. You can specify in your will, of course, that all your probate assets are to be "poured over" into your trust, but doing this subjects those assets to probate administration—which is precisely what the trust is designed to avoid.

Like a will, a living trust should be prepared by a lawyer experienced in estate planning, whose preparation charge will range from $1,000 to $2,500. You may be able to reduce the cost by undertaking the tedious but basically simple chore of transferring your assets into the trust.[*] And, as in the case of your will, there is no good reason to put off its preparation. Although you won't realize the major advantage of the trust until you become disabled or die, it's just as well to set it up early in life, because disability and death are unforeseeable and because the legal costs of setting it up are likely to be no lower 10 to 20 years from now.

FEDERAL GIFT AND ESTATE TAX

You might think that the government would stop taxing you after you die, but this isn't quite the case. It may well be that on your death your estate will be subject to what is known as the Federal Gift and Estate

---

[*]In recent years, a number of books have been published that offer do-it-yourself instructions for preparing a trust document. In addition, some telemarketing firms have exploited the public (mainly the elderly) by offering trust preparation to people who have no need for it. At best, such firms overcharge their clients; at worst, they persuade them to move their assets into dubious investments on which they earn commissions.

Both the books and the telemarketers offer a one-size-fits-all trust document that consists almost entirely of "boilerplate." Because a trust must be carefully tailored to your specific needs, you should not rely on these sources for preparation of a trust document.

Tax. Because this tax applies only to estates with a taxable value of more than $600,000, you may feel that it's unlikely to affect you. But if you bear in mind that this tax also applies to nonprobate assets such as life insurance proceeds and assets held in joint ownership or a revocable living trust, as well as to some of the gifts you make during your lifetime, you may have second thoughts. In any event, understanding how the tax works can help you soften its impact on your survivors if not avoid it entirely.

Basically this Gift and Estate Tax provides you with an initial exemption of $600,000, which can be understood more easily if you regard it as a lifetime "line of credit." Against this credit you will be "charged" with (1) the value of all gifts of more than $3,000 (or $6,000 if made with the consent of your spouse) that you made to any one individual in any one year before 1982, (2) the value of all gifts of more than $10,000 ($20,000 if made with the consent of your spouse) that you made to any individual in any one year after 1981, and (3) the value of your taxable estate after your death. Thus if, during 1987, you and your spouse made gifts of $50,000 to each of your three children, you will have used up $90,000 of your "credit," and your estate will be taxed to the extent that its value exceeds $510,000. If you made no such taxable gifts, your estate will be tax-exempt up to the value of $600,000.

One way to avoid this tax completely is to leave your entire estate to your spouse, because spouses enjoy an unlimited marital deduction. But this tactic may have some disadvantages, and at best it may postpone rather than solve the death-tax problem because her estate will be taxable on her death unless she reduces it to $600,000, or remarries and leaves everything to a surviving spouse. A second tax-reduction device involves a type of trust by which a husband and wife can leave up to $1,200,000 to children uneroded by the $235,000 in taxes that otherwise would be assessed. But readers who accumulate such wealth are likely to seek estate-planning advice that goes far beyond the scope of this book. There are, however, a couple of immediately usable strategies that can reduce your taxable estate.

Assigning Your Insurance Policies

Because the proceeds of your life insurance policies are included in the value of your estate for estate-tax purposes, one way to reduce the total value is to assign the policies to someone else—usually the beneficiary—simply by executing an assignment form obtainable from your insurance company. The recipient becomes responsible for paying the premiums and has the right to change the beneficiaries and to cash in the policy or borrow against it, but this should constitute no risk if the recipient is the beneficiary or some other trusted person.

There are two potential problems with this tactic, one foreseeable, the other not. First, if the *cash surrender value* (not the face value) of the assigned policies exceeds $10,000/$20,000, the assignment may constitute a taxable gift and thus defeat its purpose. Second, if you die within three years of making the assignment, this strategy won't work because the life insurance proceeds will be counted as part of your taxable estate.

"Gifting off" Your Assets

Because the government can't tax you on what you don't own, the simplest tactic for reducing the value of your taxable estate is to give some of it away during your lifetime. But, although you have probably made numerous cash gifts of moderate size to your children—perhaps in the form of custodial accounts—the notion of making large gifts that significantly reduce your own net worth may strike you as somewhat bizarre. Nevertheless, if you reach late middle age with assets and a pension plan sufficient to meet your retirement needs and any intervening emergencies, "gifting off" some of your assets to your children can serve several purposes. First, it will immediately reduce the income tax you pay on their yield. Second, if you make each child annual gifts totaling less than $10,000 (or $20,000 with the consent of your spouse), the gifts are not subject to any tax. Third, by the time of your death these gifts may have reduced the value of your estate below the $600,000 taxable minimum.

But perhaps the greatest advantage of such gifts during your lifetime is that they may provide your children with assets at a time when they genuinely need them (for your grandchildren's college education, for example) and they permit the recipients to express their gratitude while you are still around to enjoy it.

INDEX